IT'S A DOC'S LIFE

It's A Doc's Life gives an unusual, revealing and
funny insight into the training which a future
doctor undergoes at medical school – as seen
through the eyes of one of Britain's best-known
'media doctors'.

Alternately funny and tragic, his true story of
how he trained as a doctor will be welcomed by
his many readers and TV viewers – and should
also appeal to a whole new audience, who will
appreciate this devastatingly frank and controver-
sial inside view of the medical profession.

About the author

Dr David Delvin is Consultant Editor of *General Practitioner* and Medical Consultant to the Family Planning Association. He has appeared in hundreds of radio and television programmes, and has been Medical Adviser to such TV programmes as *Pebble Mill at One, Medical Express, Inside Medicine, The Afternoon Programme, Aspel and Company* and *About Anglia*.

He writes regular columns for national magazines and for various journals. His books, which include THE BOOK OF LOVE, HOW TO IMPROVE YOUR SEX LIFE and THE DELVIN REPORT ON SAFER SEX, published by NEL, have been translated into eight languages and one has won the Best Book Award of The American Medical Writers' Association. He recently won the 'Consumer Columnist of the Year' award, and was awarded the *Médaille de la Ville de Paris* by Jacques Chirac for highly discreet services to France.

Dr David Delvin has three grown-up children and is now married to the TV presenter and novelist Christine Webber.

IT'S A
DOC'S
LIFE

Dr David Delvin

NEW ENGLISH LIBRARY
Hodder and Stoughton

First published in Great Britain in
1990 by New English
Library paperbacks

A New English Library
paperback original

British Library C.I.P.
Delvin,   David.
 It's a doc's life
 1. Great Britain. Medicine – Biographies
 I. Title
 610.92

ISBN 0-450-50252-X

Printed and bound in Great Britain
for Hodder and Stoughton
Paperbacks, a division of Hodder and
Stoughton Ltd., Mill Road,
Dunton Green, Sevenoaks, Kent
TN13 2YA.
(Editorial Office: 47 Bedford Square,
London, WC1B 3DP) by Cox & Wyman
Reading, Berkshire. Typeset by Hewer
Text Composition Services, Edinburgh

Dedicated with affection to the memory of my uncle Freddy Hoar ('Unk') – who was a scholar, a gent, and a friend to all.

Acknowledgments

Thanks to Christina Roe and Valerie Woods for their help in preparing the manuscript; also to Alastair Delvin for finding the missing bits, and to Brian Lee of *Titbits* for digging out the press cuttings of my medical student days.

Contents

Introduction

Medicine is not all laughs.

In fact, a lot of the time, it's sheer, bloody tragedy. Like many doctors, I've found that the only way to cope with a life in medicine is to try and retain a sense of humour among all the gore and disaster.

Because if you didn't laugh, you'd weep – or else crack up (which is actually what quite a few doctors do).

So, dear reader: please forgive the eccentric – and often grim – style of humour in this book.

It's what's kept me sane – or at least, *relatively* sane – these last thirty years or so.

Dr David Delvin

PS: I've changed a number of names of people, places and hospitals, in order to protect patients' confidentiality – and also to avoid expensive libel actions. (The cheap ones I can handle.)

Nonetheless, what follows is the truth, and without any element of exaggeration. Any doc will tell you that a life in the medical profession is so full of bizarre and hysterically unpredictable incidents that there's no need for a memoirist to indulge in the slightest spot of the old hyperbole. Read on!

A MEDICAL STUDENT'S TRAINING

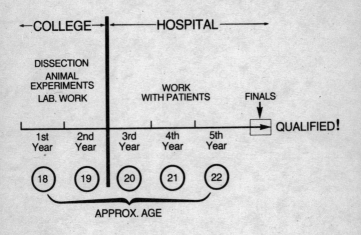

1

WHY DO YOU WANT TO BE A DOCTOR?

THE ONE THING that always brings back the recollection of my first day at medical school is the smell of preserved dead bodies.

It's funny how smell has this power to revive old memories. I think the olfactory centres of the brain are supposed to be connected with the cerebral memory circuits – though I may well have been away from anatomy class on the day we did that bit. But perhaps you've noticed how a nostrilful of the aroma of fish and chips can instantly produce the recollection of early childhood holidays. Or, more romantically, you may have noticed that the faintest whiff of a certain perfume (or a certain aftershave, I suppose) can suddenly conjure up the sensation of being in the arms – p'raps even the armpits – of a particular lover of long ago.

Anyway, for me the smell which evokes that first, frightening day at medical school is the strange half-meaty, half-antiseptic aroma of the dissecting room. One whiff of *that* particular mixture and I'm back again in the great, gloomy corridor of the anatomy department of my medical college: a scared, diffident eighteen-year-old in an ill-fitting Harris tweed suit.

And I'm casting a *very* nervous eye at the frosted glass doors which lead to the vast dissecting room – doors which are only slightly ajar, but ajar enough to release that cloying odour, and ajar enough to give a glimmer of the pale, pasty horrors that await within: the 'bods'.

Now, in theory, a boy or girl should be delighted at being on the very threshold of a medical career. *I was simply terrified*.

And some of the other lads and lasses who stood in the corridor outside the dissecting room with me were a trifle uneasy too. The knowledge that they were about to start cutting up human bodies made several of them try to cover up their feelings with the sort of excessively hearty jesting for which I'm afraid medical students are famous. Remarks like 'It's going to be a *stiff* test, this', and 'I'm not *dead* sure I want to be a doctor after all' bounced off the cold, tiled walls along with harsh and slightly desperate laughter.

But I noted with surprise that some of the straight-out-of-school youngsters seemed to be totally unmoved by the fact that, in a couple of minutes, they'd be dismembering human corpses. I wondered if these tough characters were the sort of callous brutes who'd have made highly efficient concentration-camp doctors. Or were they just totally and utterly devoid of imagination?

In fact, in the course of the next few years, I was to discover that many of those 'tough' or 'unimaginative' boys and girls could be badly upset or frightened or embarrassed by other aspects of medicine – aspects which (much to my surprise) didn't bother me at all. Sex, for instance . . .

Anyway, I'm glad to say that although a few of the eighteen-year-olds who were gathered in the anatomy corridor that morning turned out to be the kind of big-headed, sexist snobs who get medicine a bad name, many others – far from being insensitive or unfeeling – did eventually mature into decent, kind and conscientious doctors.

On the other hand, my opinion – for what it's worth – is that the training we went through during those next few years did have a strong brutalizing element in it; it also tended to induce in us the arrogant feeling that we were somehow 'a breed apart'.

See what you think.

*   *   *

But first, you may possibly wonder how we all came to be standing in that glum, smelly corridor on that gloomy day in the late 1950s. How had we got into the college at all?

In those days (just like today) the competition for medical school places was very tough indeed. I'd sent applications to several colleges when I was about sixteen, but my prospects of getting into any of them didn't seem too good, mainly because I knew next to nothing about the scientific subjects in which schoolboys and schoolgirls are supposed to be thoroughly grounded if they want to be accepted on the course for a medical degree.

My attempt to get into Cambridge without any serious knowledge of science struck the dons of St John's College as a jest in only moderate taste – and I must say I had to agree with them. I spent a few pleasant days 'in college' sitting the Cambridge scholarship exam, but came away with little more than a new-found knowledge of the traditional St John's limerick (said to have been penned by Oliver St John Gogarty):

> *There was a young man of St John's*
> *Who wanted to roger the swans;*
> *But the old college porter*
> *Said 'No – take my daughter!*
> *Them swans is reserved for the dons.'*

Soon afterwards (aged about seventeen), I was given an interview at the Wessex Hospital Medical School – an interview which consisted of ten minutes in a large, dark, grim room with a large, dark, grim doctor whose manner suggested that he was trying to find some way of informing a terminal patient that the case was hopeless. The interview reached its lowest depths when he asked me the standard question: '*Why do you really want to be a doctor?*'

I had no ready reply to this – which was decidedly unwise of me, to put it mildly! I think I muttered something about 'wanting to help people' – which certainly did *not* seem to go down well at all with the dark, grim doctor.

I didn't get in.

So I'd advise any would-be medical students who're reading this book to have an answer prepared for *that* particular (and almost inevitable) question. Without any adequate reply, you're most unlikely to get a place at medical school.

And don't make the mistake of the young man who, when asked why he wanted to be a doctor, replied 'Because I have long fingers, sir . . .'

*   *   *

In fact, the *real* reason why I was trying to get into medicine wasn't awfully likely to appeal to an interview board. It was this.

My parents had forced me into it. And despite the fact that I was a strong-willed boy who was only too ready to defy authority on points of principle, I'd eventually given in to my Mum and Dad's pressure to choose medicine — right back when I was only thirteen or fourteen.

My parents' reason for driving me into a medical career was odd but, in a sad way, understandable. Let me explain.

My mother – a charming but dotty early Celtic feminist, who originated from half-way up a mountain in County Kerry – had been desperately ill for years with a kidney disease. Throughout my childhood, my parents seemed to be on a never-ending tour of the London teaching hospitals, trying to find a cure for her. There was none. Touchingly – though quite daftly – my Mum seemed to believe that if she could only get me into a teaching hospital and qualified as a doctor, *I* might be the one to find the answer to her illness.

So, as a very young teenager, I'd been loony enough to give in to the massive pressure exerted by her and my father. It seemed to be my filial duty to study scientific subjects at school, regardless of the fact that I wasn't actually much *good* at science. (BANG! . . . 'Was that you again, Delvin?' . . . 'Yessir.' . . . 'Then you must pay for the damage, foolish boy!')

I was mainly interested in books, writing, sport, opera and (oh, yes) girls, but *not* in science – except, of course, for the fascinating bits of science which related to girls. . . .

F'rinstance, in the school biology lab we learned that the female rabbit had something called a clitoris, and wondered desperately if a girl had one, and if it would be in much the same place. Indeed, on one of the school's educational visits abroad – a visit whose educational content seemed to be mainly confined to romantic encounters on moonlit beaches – I actually heard a hoarse seventeen-year-old male voice whispering, 'Could you tell me where your clitoris is? I'm afraid I'm working on *Grove & Newell's Textbook of Animal Biology* from here upwards.'

As far as I am aware, the young lady didn't know where her clitoris was either – which is fairly symptomatic of the fog of sexual ignorance which covered the world in the mid-1950s.

Later, back in the school biology lab we had another look at *Grove & Newell's Textbook of Animal Biology* and also at *Gray's Anatomy* and confirmed that a female bunny's *cli-cli* was, indeed, where a girl's is – namely, at the front. This was totally confusing, when you consider the way rabbits make love – i.e., the other way round from us.

So what on earth was this intriguing little button *for*?

No biological or medical textbook of those days offered any explanation whatever for its existence. But we did have access to American women's magazines which hinted darkly that 'orgasm derived from stimulating the clitoris is highly *immature*, and should not be encouraged, since the proper orgasm is vaginal orgasm.'

Goodness! So you could stimulate it – *that* was what you could do with it! And you could cause an orgasm with it – even if it was an 'immature' one.

Now if you bear in mind that (as sixth formers intending to study medicine) we knew far more about sex than ninety-nine per cent of young British men, you can imagine the total and utter sexual cluelessness of the average bloke at that time.

And even in the 1960s and 1970s (when I began to work in the field of sex medicine), I found that a very high proportion of husbands hadn't a notion of where the clitoris was, or what to do with it. (And very often, they couldn't have cared less. . . .)

Anyway, I was extremely fortunate in that round about 1956 A Naughty Book was secretly passed around the biology sixth. (We'd have been in enormous trouble if we'd been caught with it.) It was *The Green Light*, a simple and honest guide to sexual medicine, written for the public by a chap called René MacAndrew.

Frankly, I think the guy should have been canonized. He wasn't a doctor, yet he'd managed to get down on paper all the important information that was available at that time about how to have a gentle, loving, tender sexual relationship between a man and a woman. If you're still alive, René, thank you very much, *mon brave*!

Anyway, his sensible words made clear to us that the clitoris was actually the main key to female sexual satisfaction – and that if we wanted to make our future wives happy, we'd better learn how to *use* that key.

He had nothing to say on the subject of rabbits, so I'm afraid I still don't know why the female bunny's *Kitzler* (as they say in Germany) is at the front. If there are any psychosexual zoologists (or, indeed, any rabbits) reading this book, I'd be grateful if they'd write in and let me know.

Well, now, talking about rabbits, I have to admit that in

school dissection classes I was physically sick when we had to do in and cut up the unlucky bunnies. Dissection was *not* my strong suit. Faced with the necessity to dissect a dogfish and report my results, I gave up and wrote a poem, chiefly in the Scottish dialect, in honour of the unfortunate creature. Not surprisingly, this kind of behaviour tended to bring me about six per cent in my end-of-term exams – which hardly suggested that I was cut out for medicine.

Now when I was seventeen, my poor old Mum's kidneys gave up the unequal struggle – a struggle in which the medical knowledge of those days could do little to aid them. Inevitably, she finished her life in yet another London teaching hospital (I think it was about her seventh).

Really, any boy with any sense would have realised that this was the moment to forget about applying for a place at medical school. However, I mistakenly thought that I'd now gone too far to turn back. Furthermore, my father – an extremely forceful and determined Scotsman – made clear to me that a life in the healing arts was what Mum had most wanted for me. He implied that she was now on high, waiting for me to take the Royal College of Surgeons by storm, and was probably regaling the angels with tales of how her son was going to win the Nobel prize for medicine.

Another factor which stopped me from giving up and going into a safe profession (like journalism or poetry) was this. My poor old Dad was quite ill as well. A wild, crazy, romantic man who'd been a superb athlete in his youth, he'd been hit very hard (both physically and emotionally) by diabetes.

Diabetes is a fascinating disease in which patient and doctor have to strive hard to achieve a delicate balance – a balance between the body's level of insulin, and the body's level of sugar.

Unfortunately, 'balance' was not a word which existed in my Dad's vocabulary. Despite his diabetes, he continued to try to live life to the full – playing thirty-six holes of golf a day, taking me on in quarter-mile and half-mile races, driving himself to the limit at his work (he was a superb teacher), and skimping on his meals.

The inevitable result was that he had frequent attacks of very low blood sugar – which make a diabetic first of all confused and irritable, and then unconscious. The remedy (if you can apply it fast enough) is just to get the patient to eat some food.

After my Mum died, my Dad became liable to wild attacks of nocturnal confusion brought on by low blood sugar. These attacks had a kind of crazy surrealistic atmosphere, reminiscent of Thurber's story *The Night the Bed Fell on Father*.

For instance, one morning I was awoken at about 2 a.m. by loud crashes from my father's bedroom. I went in, and found him practising his golf shots. Very roughly, the following dialogue ensued:

ME:	Hey, what're you doing?
FATHER:	I'm just getting ready – I've got to be on the first tee in half an hour. (CRASH!)
ME:	For heaven's sake, it's the middle of the night!
FATHER:	No it isn't, boy. I know what time it is! (CRASH!)
ME:	Look, your blood sugar's low. Let me get you some grub.
FATHER:	Nonsense! (CRASH!) I'll just get my plus-fours on and I'll be off to the course. I must remember to keep the head doon today . . . (CRASH!)

There was no reasoning with him. He insisted on getting dressed for golf, so I went downstairs and prepared a couple of cheese sandwiches. Just before he tore out the front door with his gear, I prevailed on him to eat them 'to give you strength for the match.'

The effect – as always – was magical. Two or three

minutes after starting to eat the sandwiches, sanity suddenly displaced confusion in his eyes as the food supplies reached his brain. He looked in amazement at his clothes and his bag, and then realised what had happened.

'Oh God, it was ma blood sugar again . . . Sorry about that . . . Thanks for looking after me . . .'

On some occasions I didn't get there with the sandwiches or sugar-lumps in time, and he was carted off unconscious to hospital. On one or two nights he was picked up by the police who understandably thought he was drunk. But most times I caught him with a packet of biscuits or a cheese roll before he drifted off into the unrousable slumber of low blood sugar.

These bizarre nights were actually quite useful training for my later career – when I qualified as a doctor, I was pleasantly relieved to find that the 'cheese roll treatment' worked on other diabetics too!

You can see that at the age of seventeen, I didn't want to upset the poor, bereaved guy any further by refusing to go along with his wish that I train as a doctor. And even more potent was the memory of my poor old mother, with whose constantly worsening illness I had lived through most of my childhood. The idea that if I were a doctor, I might *cure* that kind of illness was very strong in me.

Crazy though it all sounds, the fact is that feelings like that are very hard to resist when you're seventeen, and when you're also in a state of some shock at the recent departure of your Mum to the Great Teaching Hospital in the Sky. So – I complied, and continued with my efforts to be accepted by a medical school.

It wasn't until thirty years later that I realised that all that early parental conditioning had 'programmed' me to want passionately to help sick and troubled women – and that *that* was why I eventually took up 'agony aunt' and contraceptive work, and ended up trying to help women with sexual and gynaecological problems. This dotty life-long desire to help females in distress also led me into one or two fairly disastrous amatory adventures (though not, thank God, with patients!).

*   *   *

But to return to the 1950s: having failed to get into Cambridge and the Wessex Hospital, I had only one medical school interview left. It was at Queen's College, London, where they were said to accept only one applicant in twenty-three – so my chances of a medical career were looking a trifle rickety, to say the least.

Still, I went along to the interview – crammed into a terrible old check suit of my father's, which made me look like an acromegalic bookie (and a remarkably unsuccessful acromegalic bookie, at that). The suit itself should have been enough to kill off my medical career.

Yet how strange life is! I got into the interview room, and faced a panel of four middle-aged men who were clearly bored to tears from grilling countless applicants all day long for a week or so.

For some extraordinary reason, I promptly cracked a joke, and then exchanged a few pleasantries with a Celtic doctor who'd recognised in me the racial characteristics of the Irish (especially the broken nose and cauliflower ear). Somehow or other, I made them laugh.

Five minutes later, I shambled out of the room in my ridiculous suit, leaving behind a bunch of blokes who were at least amused at having encountered anyone quite so potty on a hot and tedious afternoon.

On such mad inconsequentialities are careers founded. The eccentric, sputtering sparks which were struck between me and the interview panel that day were to decide the pattern of my life. Shortly afterwards, they wrote me a note offering me a place at Queen's College, London, which I thought was uncommonly decent of them.

Come to think of it, they hadn't even asked me 'Why do you want to be a doctor?'

2

CUTTING UP THE DEAD

AT ALL BRITISH medical schools (except for a couple of the newer ones, which have more enlightened ideas), you spend your first eighteen or twenty-four months without ever seeing a real live patient. Instead, you study the so-called 'pre-clinical' subject of anatomy and physiology. A lot of guys regarded the pre-clinical period as the happiest of their lives. I did not. The main reason for this was . . . dissection.

Rabbits and dogfish had been bad enough, but *humans* . . . ugh!

In the early part of my first term of anatomy, I was sitting on the back seat of the top of a London bus, mugging up on my newly-acquired dissection manual. A very loud and very nosy woman came and sat down next to me.

'Couldn't help seeing the title of that book you're reading, dear,' she said, so that the rest of the top deck heard her. '*Handbook of Dissection*, is it? You're a medical student, aren't you? And what do you dissect, then?'

'Er . . . dead bodies.'

'Ah, yes . . . well, I can see you're not well off, dear, so I suppose you *have* to make do with cutting up dead bodies. But if you were one of those *rich* students, they'd let you cut up live people, wouldn't they?'

Such staggering misunderstandings were, and probably

still are, common among the non-medical public – or 'the *lay* public', in the amazingly pompous phrase that our instructors soon taught us.

For instance, when I first started at Queen's College, London, WC2, in that autumn term of 1957, my girl-friend's Mum was appalled to think that I was about to spend a couple of years or so in carving up dead humans.

'I thought you medical students all practised on wax dummies,' she said in the horror-struck tones of someone who's just been told that her potential son-in-law is a necrophiliac.

But no – they *weren't* wax dummies. On that first October morning when we walked through the big glass doors of the dissecting room and sniffed the awful corpsey smell, it was all too clear that our 'subjects' (as the lecturers called them) had once been human beings.

On twenty-four glass tables, arranged in neat rows, twenty-four naked bodies lay staring at the high ceiling, like victims of some small but rigidly organised Belsen.

Oddly enough, it was their nakedness that shocked me most: I can still see the limp, dead breasts, the pathetic tufts of pubic hair pointing skywards, and the poor, tired penises that would never exercise either of their natural functions again.

We sat down at the glass tables with our anatomy manuals and our little dissection kits of knives and tweezers. Two other blokes and I were assigned to spend the next term exploring one arm of our 'subject'. Three other students were to work on his opposite arm; three on each of his legs, three on his head and neck; and three on his thorax and abdomen. You have to admit it: that left the poor man fairly fully occupied. To defuse our fear of him, we called him 'Fred'.

* * *

Now how the heck had Fred and his heavily embalmed companions got there in the first place?

Well, one large group of the dead were paupers. They'd died so poor that there wasn't enough cash to pay for a funeral – so the Government had turned their frail cadavers over to the anatomy department for dissection by us medical students.

I suppose that sounds pretty hideous, doesn't it? But our 'demonstrators' (young doctors who taught us the carving techniques) told us that this was a very *good* arrangement really, because it meant that the poor souls 'would eventually get a Christian burial.'

I wasn't wildly impressed with this argument – because what actually happened to the paupers' bodies was this.

They lay on the glass tables for a year or so, while the medical students systematically picked their bones clean, leaving little more than skeletons. But all the 'bits' which had come off the bones (skin, muscles, tendons, stomachs, hearts, brains, livers, kidneys, whatever) were swept away at the end of each day's dissection into a revoltingly greasy tray at the end of each glass table. From there, it all went into a sort of communal fleshpot in another room, where the 'scraps' of twenty-four dead people were kept in storage for many months while their owners were still being dissected.

It's true that at the end of all this time – when we'd all finished our dissection course – the two dozen skeletons would be interred with a simple chapel service (which, to their great credit, a few of the more religious medical students took the trouble to attend). But what struck me as bizarre – and rather demeaning to the poor 'subjects' – was the fact that once a skeleton had been placed in each coffin, it was simply filled up with a random selection of material from the half-ton bin of fleshy bits which had been swept up each day, derived from the bodies of Fred, and Jim, and Mary, and Vera, and Bill . . .

In other words, *your* coffin with *your* name on it would contain just your bones – plus no more than one-twenty-fourth of your flesh, all muddled up with bits from the other twenty-three bodies in the dissection room! The ultimate in togetherness, really.

For some reason, it seemed to me that this matey arrangement was particularly unfair to the other group of 'donors' of bodies.

You see, not all our 'subjects' were paupers. Many were the corpses of people who'd generously willed their bodies 'for medical research'.

I've always admired men and women who do this. I still encounter them today, and indeed they quite often write to me at my 'agony aunt' columns asking for the address where they can get forms to leave their bodies 'for research'.

I feel that they're very decent people who – quite understandably – imagine that the donation of their bodies will be warmly welcomed by research scientists who're searching for, perhaps, a possible cure for cancer.

('Great news, Dr Fortescue – someone's left us a body *for research*.' 'Tremendous, Carruthers! This could be the breakthrough we've been waiting for!')

Well, I doubted in 1957 – and I doubt still – whether many of these good-hearted donors realised that their final destiny was to be sliced up by a batch of young medics – and then to have their shredded flesh mixed up with the *disjecta* of two dozen other bodies.

You *could* call that 'medical research', I suppose, but it did seem to me a curious twisting of the term – perhaps 'medical education' would have been more honest.

It was all a bit symptomatic of the way that we were already being encouraged to feel that there were certain things which there was no need for the public (sorry, the *lay* public) to know; things which should only be discussed by a privileged élite – namely ourselves.

Certainly, digging about deep in people's bodies and finding out the secrets of their anatomy did inevitably tend to give us the arrogant feeling that we were (please forgive the phrase) a cut above the rest of humanity.

As you'll have gathered, it also gave *me* a feeling of utter revulsion! My first incision into poor smelly old Fred's arm, to try and expose his muscles and nerves, was one of the most unpleasant experiences of my eighteen-year-old life. I can still feel my knife going through the tough, grey skin to reveal the yellow, squishy fat below – all far too reminiscent of something you find on the edge of a plate of Irish stew. . . .

In the early weeks, I found it very hard to adopt the hearty, to-hell-with-it attitude which many of the other students rapidly developed. Indeed, during the first three days of the long, long dissection course, I actually felt I had to go out to the pub at lunch-time and down a neat brandy to steady my nerves (and how I afforded three shillings for *that* on my student grant, I don't know).

It was many months before I gradually got used to the process of dissection – and several more months than that before I could face the all-too-evocative lunch-time steak and kidney pie in the college refectory. In fact, if it hadn't been for my girl-friend (a buxom, kindly lass who knew how to solace a badly-worried medical student), I don't think I'd have completed that endless stint in the dissection room. In the soft warmth of her bosom, I was able to forget the distress of the day.

*   *   *

But eventually I acquired a bit of the tough gallows humour that has helped protect the fragile emotions of generations of medical students – from stately, plump Buck Mulligan to, I suppose, Dr Crippen.

(Crippen was actually a dentist, not a doctor – but dentists do dissection too, though only as far down as the waist. Your local dental surgeon is absolutely brilliant on the anatomy of anything from the top of your head down to your ribs. But below your navel, he's *lost*. Ladies: never take a dentist for a lover.)

In short, we were all becoming hard as nails about death,

and the means by which most of us did it was to make a bit of a joke of it. 'Good-morning, Fred,' we'd say when we arrived in the dissecting room. 'Hope you haven't been taking any dead liberties during the night.'

However, I still found it very hard to sympathise with the medics who found the whole thing so hilarious that they'd laughingly pick up a piece of someone's flesh and throw it at a colleague on the other side of the 'DR'.

And I felt frankly revolted when one of my dissecting partners (nowadays, a staid, respectable, middle-aged doctor in the field of industrial medicine) suddenly opened his trouser zip while walking down the corridor and showed the rest of us a curious cylindrical brown object which, on close inspection, turned out to be not his penis but an illicitly-removed human forefinger.

In fairness to the college, I must say that the authorities did their best to forbid this kind of thing and to try and instil in us some respect for the 'subjects'. The dead digit in the trouser-fly wasn't their fault – and with the hindsight of thirty years, I can see that the boy who played this grim jape probably did it because it was his defence against the unpleasantness of day after day spent cutting up the dead.

*   *   *

Now, is there really any point in making medical students undergo the long and rather disgusting task of dissecting cadavers?

I suppose there is, because it's almost certainly the best way of implanting the main points of anatomical knowledge forever in one's memory. On the other hand, it seems to me to be a training which is a bit brutalizing in itself. Moreover, the sheer length of the course makes it more appropriate to a future surgeon than to, say, a future GP or a future paediatrician – both of whom might perhaps be better employed in learning about human relationships and communication, subjects which were (and still are) disastrously neglected in the medical course.

In fact, many of the boys (and some of the girls) who started in the anatomy department with me in 1957 did go on to become surgeons – so the long months of dissection were no doubt a help to them in their careers.

But as for me – well, I realised one morning quite early on in my dissection course that I was far too manually clumsy to be a surgeon.

This revelation came to me one day when I grasped poor old Fred's little finger and attempted to move it a few inches sideways. To my extreme embarrassment, the entire finger suddenly broke off in my hand. My partners unsuccessfully tried to stick it back on with Sellotape, in the hope that the demonstrators wouldn't notice. (They did.)

All I can say in defence of my own clumsiness is that, thirty years later, I haven't broken any bits off any other patient.

At least, not yet.

3

DOING IN THE ANIMALS

BY NOW YOU'LL certainly have gathered that I found the first couple of years at medical school a trifle grim, to say the least – mainly because the long process of dissection of pickled bodies was so unpleasant.

But dissection wasn't *all* we did in those first two years (though it sometimes seemed like it). We actually studied three main subjects:

anatomy;

physiology; and

pharmacology.

Curiously enough, the trio of professors who taught us these three subjects were all Scotsmen, a fact which helped to confirm my already-solid belief in the intellectual pre-eminence of the Caledonian race.

Anatomy didn't just consist of the drudgery of the dissecting room: there were also anatomy *lectures*, which I personally found a great deal pleasanter, because the great amphitheatre of the lecture room was several yards from the 'DR' – and therefore free of its sickly smell.

Some anatomy lectures were on *osteology* – the study of bones. You have about 212 bones in your body (more if you've been eating kippers), and we were supposed to learn every bump on every single one of them.

The osteology lectures were delivered by a pompous

19

young doctor who we regarded with considerable interest, mainly because it was rumoured throughout the college that he'd recently been a victim of the condition known as *penis captivus*. This is the alleged disorder in which a gent becomes 'entrapped' inside a lady during love-making, because of a powerful spasm of her vaginal muscles, which in effect refuse to let him out.

I call it an 'alleged' disorder because of the fact that, in half a lifetime of practice since then, I've never seen a case nor even met anyone who's seen one. However, when I expressed this cynical view in a medical journal a few years ago, I received half a dozen letters from doctors who claimed to have heard of entwined and embarrassed couples walking 'four-legged' into Casualty, demanding to be released from this bizarre involuntary fusion! I'm afraid I still don't believe them.

Anyway, Dr O'Carroll (the osteologist) was supposed to have been carried into his own teaching hospital's accident department, accompanied on the stretcher by a petrified nurse who was – so to speak – 'as one' with him. Most of us fervently believed the story (which gained greatly in the telling on our way home from rugby matches) that Dr O'C and his nurse friend had remained inseparable until freezing cold ethyl chloride local anaesthetic had been sprayed – with some difficulty – on to their combined personal parts.

The fact that we readily believed this dotty story about Dr O'Carroll was, I suppose, a measure of our general sexual ignorance. You may be surprised to learn that at no time in our medical training did we ever receive any teaching about sex at all – a crazy situation when you consider that so many of the problems which take people to doctors' surgeries are connected with sex in some way.

We were taught where the various 'naughty bits' were, and that was about it! There was no question whatever of telling us how they *worked*.

Maybe our instructors themselves didn't really know – or

maybe they just hoped we'd pick it all up somehow by experimentation with willing partners in our spare time. The result of all this was that those few students who remained virgins during the whole of their training were eventually launched on the public as qualified doctors in a state of total and utter absence of any knowledge whatever about sex!

Once again, I was lucky. In the deep and tender relationship which I shared with my girl-friend over a period of years, we slowly and lovingly learned to cherish and to respect each other's bodies, and to give (and receive) great happiness.

It was something for which I shall always be grateful to her. Thirty years later, we are still good – though platonic – friends, and I believe it's a source of considerable amusement and satisfaction to her that so much of what we gradually learned together was eventually translated into not just a series of best-selling sex manuals, but (more importantly) into the treatment of very large numbers of patients.

Thank you, ma'am. . . .

*   *   *

Anyway, back to Dr O'Carroll, the randy osteologist.

He did his best to instil into our brains the knowledge of every groove, hole and furrow in those 212 bones – so that we'd know exactly what muscles are attached to them, and what nerves and blood vessels run over and through them.

In fact, in order to learn this sort of thing you needed to have your own personal skeleton to work on in the evenings. So, like all medical students for the last 150 years or so, every one of us bought a box of human bones and carted them home – much to the amazement and/or horror of our landladies and families!

My personal skeleton was a pretty tatty old one, which I bought from a senior student for about twelve quid. Soon after I got it home, I discovered that I was violently allergic to something in it – probably tiny dust mites which had taken up residence in the small crevices of the skull. (Lots of people are allergic to dust mites, but don't know it.) As a result, I started sneezing and came out in a thundering itchy rash every time I tried to do any homework on the bones. This episode was a good introduction to the whole fascinating subject of the allergy, but did make it *just* a trifle difficult for me to pass my osteology exams. . . .

You may wonder where these skeletons come from. Well, they're passed on from generation to generation of medical students, and they seem to have mainly originated in Third World countries.

Naturally, in recent years those Third World countries have grown just a *teeny* bit less than enthusiastic about shipping the bones of their less popular citizens off to western medical schools (particularly since the practice of cannibalism has grown a trifle less socially acceptable). So the supply of skeletons is slowly drying up.

As a direct result, the price of bones has been sky-rocketing, and today a medical student has to pay well over £100 for his personal skeleton. Even in my time as a student, bones were so valuable that there were occasional scandals when crooked dissecting room technicians were found to be surreptitiously extracting tibias, femurs and whatnots from the dead bodies in the anatomy department – and quietly flogging them on the black market!

Quite rightly, the college was extremely vigilant for this sort of thing, since the authorities didn't like the idea of our poor old 'subjects' being buried with only one leg or one arm.

Indeed, if any of our dissecting room technicians had been caught by our professor of anatomy in the act of knocking off bits of the dead, I daresay he'd have skinned 'em alive and pickled them in formalin.

For he was one of the most formidable and fearsome men I'd ever met: Professor Macallister, a broad, muscular, bald-headed bloke, with a voice like an Aberdeen fog-horn.

An excellent lecturer and a stern disciplinarian, Macallister waged a relentlessly successful campaign to ensure that we medical students were properly behaved and properly attired. He told us indignantly that when he'd first come to the college, 'there were actually *students wearing polo-neck sweaters*!' Well, he'd soon wiped out polo-neck sweaters, along with every other irregularity of dress. Under his awesome rule, we rapidly learned that would-be doctors should be dressed in quiet ties, unflashy shirts and conservative jackets – *or else*.

We also learned that you were punctual – or God help you! Some time very early in my long sojourn in the anatomy department, I tried to slip into the back of one of his lectures some three minutes late. I immediately found myself on the receiving end of a terrifying war-cry of 'You, laddie – you with the *beard*!' – followed by a merciless twenty minute public inquisition concerning the course of the internal carotid artery (on which I was a wee bit poorly informed, to put it mildly).

After the appalling going-over which he gave me that morning, I went straight home, shaved off my beard, changed my hairstyle, and totally altered the rather 'arty' way in which I dressed. Next day, the prof spent some time looking round the vast lecture theatre for me – but he was unable to recognise yesterday's villain in the clean-shaven, neatly-suited lad who was sitting taking assiduous notes in the third row.

The experience certainly taught me a great deal about how appearance can alter people's perceptions of other human beings! It was a lesson which has proved exceptionally useful, not only in medicine (where it's all too easy to misjudge a patient by his clothes), but also on the odd medical journalistic investigations of later years in which I've happily disguised myself as someone who couldn't *possibly* be a doctor – by the simple expedient of putting on tatty gear.

Despite the fear he inspired, Professor Macallister was

basically a kind man. Two years afterwards, he very generously helped me when I was in desperate trouble in my final anatomy practical exam – by giving me a *sotto voce* hint while I dithered over the identification of an obscure lump of brown flesh. (It turned out to be the bottom right-hand corner of somebody's heart – but you'll gather from the fact that I use the phrase 'bottom right-hand corner' that I wasn't too well up on the technical terms, like 'right ventricle'.)

Professor Macallister was also pleasant and respectful to the women medical students – at a time when they were far from warmly welcomed in all British medical schools. Some teaching hospitals had only started admitting women a few years previously, and sexist teasing of girl students by certain lecturers was quite common – especially in anatomy departments, where the opportunities for crudely embarrassing a young woman were obvious. (For instance, it was all too easy to hand a blushing girl a museum jar containing a large pair of testicles, and say 'What view d'you take of *these*, Miss Blenkinsop?')

One of those who I remember taking great delight in harassing women students at a certain medical school is now quite a fashionable surgeon, with 'Sir' in front of his name. When I last saw him, his chief pleasure in life was embarrassing young nurses in the operating theatre by making childish innuendoes about their sex lives. Nice guy, eh?

The most notorious case of sexual harassment I heard of was that of a misogynistic old lecturer who was so violently opposed to the admission of women to his particular medical school that he made a practice of beginning every teaching session with a barrage of vulgarity designed to make the female students pack up their books and leave.

It was alleged that once a year he would enter the lecture theatre with a large anatomical specimen jar containing a vast human phallus. Banging it down on the desk in front of him, he would declare, 'This gentlemen – and ladies too, of course – is the male organ of a West African who had the misfortune to be hanged. It is the finest and largest specimen of male virility known to medical science, and this morning I propose to discuss it and its sexual advantages in some detail. . . .'

At this point, the relatively delicate young women of those days would gather up their belongings and make a mass exit in protest. And as they departed through the lecture theatre doors, this charming old gent would call after them, 'Pray don't rush yourselves, ladies. The next boat for West Africa doesn't leave for a fortnight!'

I'm pleased to say that (according to my information) the tougher, gutsier women medics of the early feminist era were totally unimpressed by this kind of stuff, and rapidly drove the old chauvinist into early retirement.

P'raps he went to West Africa. . . .

*   *   *

Our 'number two' subject was physiology – the study of the workings of the human body. And I must admit that our physiology professor – Prof Macrimmon – was also a relic of a bygone age, though he too was considerate and polite to the women students, as well as to the men.

Unfortunately, he didn't have quite the same consideration for the other inhabitants of the physiology department – the poor old experimental animals.

Another Caledonian, Macrimmon was witty, entertaining, a good teacher, and the author of a guidebook to the whiskies of Scotland. One dictum of his has stayed in the minds of generations of his students: he frequently remarked that hanging was the easiest and most painless way to kill yourself, and that his friend and colleague Sir ——— ————, an expert on toxicology who knew more about drugs and their fatal dosages than anyone else in Scotland, had surprised everyone by choosing to end his life in this way.

I only had two objections to the affable professor of

physiology. One was that he made absurd efforts to promote the sales of his own famous physiology textbook (though not the whisky book) to us. Rather late in the day, I realised that it was *impossible* to get through the college physiology exams unless you knew his volume inside out – which included being able to identify the graphs which he'd produced during his own undoubtedly clever lab experiments back in the 1920s.

My other objection was that he presided over a physiology department which massacred alarmingly large numbers of animals in the course of each week of the academic year. Here again, it was a bit hard to see how all this slaughter quite fitted in with the image of the tender, caring doctors we were supposed to be developing into.*

Please make no mistake: I think that animal *research* is unfortunately necessary for the development of new drugs and (ultimately) for the saving of people's lives. But this wasn't killing for research: it was killing for *demonstration*. And in order to demonstrate some fairly useless piece of information about physiology, the prof would regularly march into the lecture theatre, clad in a purple boiler suit and followed by a lab attendant who looked a bit like a servant carrying in a boar's head on a silver salver.

Unfortunately, what he was carrying was, invariably, a half-dead cat, pegged out on some sort of tray. The professor would then do all sorts of unpleasant things to this poor old moggy's brain, to demonstrate what happened to its reflexes when parts of its nervous system were cut through.

---

* Curiously enough, it was just after I'd finished writing this chapter about the weekly massacre of animals in the physiology department that the present-day students of my old college at last 'went public' – and very bravely complained to the press about the senseless slaughter of animals which still goes on – though in reduced numbers, thanks to a recent change in the Law. At the time of writing, their campaign to reduce the number of unnecessary deaths (and to allow medical students to 'opt out' on conscience grounds) still continues. Good luck to them.

In fairness, I have to add that the pathetic animal appeared to be totally unconscious during all this. Nonetheless, my sympathies were entirely with the cruci-fied feline rather than with the prof – and, for me, the high point of the experiment was the moment when the now-dying and decerebrate cat either:

(a) lashed out with the last of his strength and scratched the professor; or

(b) peed all over him in a final superb gesture of feline defiance!

The prof spent a fair amount of time in imbuing us with propaganda against the anti-vivisection movement, whose headquarters were situated only half a mile or so from the college, at Trafalgar Square. Rather surprisingly, he urged us to go down there without revealing that we were medical students, and to ask them for large quantities of their literature – which, he said (with rather less than his usual level of wit), would make very good toilet paper.

I suppose he thought that by getting us to do this, he was somehow helping to deplete the anti-vivisection move-ment's finances. Maybe he was right – because I'm ashamed to say that quite a lot of us did indeed go and ask for the society's leaflets and posters. We didn't use them as loo paper (they were far too tough for that), but we did make cruel fun of them by sticking them on the walls of the physiology department and writing silly, thoughtless jokes on them.

Although (to my shame) I joined in all this officially-approved buffoonery, I was almost as unhappy about what we were doing in the physiology department as I was about our necrophiliac activities in the dissecting room.

In particular, each week we had a long 'physiology practical' session which occupied a full afternoon. During each of those afternoons, we were expected to carry out and report on an experiment. And, alas, all too often the experiments involved the deaths of fairly large numbers of unfortunate animals: dogs, rabbits, cats and frogs.

Right at the beginning of our two years, we were taught how to 'deal with' frogs for these experiments – and squeamish readers should *definitely* skip the next paragraph altogether.

To my immense distaste, I found that we were expected to grab the poor old frog by its hind legs, and then swing it through the air and bash its head on the side of a sink in order to stun it. Once this was done, we were supposed to stick a sharp needle-like probe through the top of its head, and so more or less demolish most of its brain. This left the unlucky frog still alive for experimentation on its beating heart (or whatever) but – I fervently hoped – unconscious. I still shudder at the recollection of the droves of frogs who perished at our hands during those two bizarre years.

But the larger animals on which we experimented were not – thank God – killed by us. The slaughter (or 'sacrifice' as we were taught to call it) of cats and dogs was carried out by slightly older medical students who did in the unlucky animals behind closed doors while we waited outside in the corridor.

One of these senior students, who was a friend of mine, told me that the worst thing about gassing or rabbit-chopping these poor creatures to death was the fact that he'd usually grown quite attached to them during the days or weeks that they'd been living in cages in the physiology department before they were 'sacrificed'.

What I found particularly stupid was the fact that most of these animal experiments which we carried out were really *a complete waste of time*. None of them – as far as I can remember – was ever of the slightest use to me as a doctor when I eventually qualified.

Much more interesting were the experiments we did on ourselves – measuring our breathing capacity, our heart rates, the way our eyes and ears worked, and the strength and fatiguability of our muscles. And many of these 'do-it-yourself' experiments were really far more valuable and informative to future doctors than messing around with half-dead cats.

For instance, a very simple one which you can do yourself is this. Press the tip of your finger firmly against the skin just next to your eye so that you're putting pressure on the side of your eyeball. You'll immediately notice that a black disc with a yellow 'surround' appears in your field of vision – on the opposite side to the one which you're pressing. This shows:

(a) that the retina – the screen at the back of your eye – can be stimulated by touch as well as by light;

(b) that it extends right round to the side of your eyeball; and

(c) that the image it produces is *reversed* – in other words, that a stimulus on the right side of the eyeball produces a picture on the other side.

All of this basic knowledge is actually of some help in treating people with eye disorders.

Another useful DIY experiment (which I would NOT advise you to try yourself) was virtually forced on us by our stroppy Irish biochemistry lecturer. In his youth, he'd quite rightly been appalled by the casual way in which doctors forced patients to swallow stomach tubes. So he insisted that all of *us* swallow these little gastric tubes, and then suck out our own stomach juices and test them to prove they were acid!

A pretty grotty experience, but it taught every one of us that you didn't just stuff a rubber tube down a patient's throat and cheerfully assume that it was causing him or her no distress whatever. . . .

*   *   *

Similarly, the professor of pharmacology (a pleasant Edinburgh man whose job it was to teach us about the effects of medicines) insisted that we do a practical experiment on laxatives – on ourselves!

'It is indeed fortunate,' he said, 'that in this particular

investigation, the experimenter and the experimental subject can be combined in one and the same person.'

Quite so.

After an uncomfortable fortnight trying out every major purgative from senna pods (ugh!) to Glauber's salts (yuk!) – and recording the horrendous results in our notebooks – we had at least learned enough about 'opening medicines' (and spent enough time on the loo) to make us think twice before dishing them out in large quantities to our future patients.

But was I ever going to get as far as the stage of *seeing* any patients? I really began to doubt it, because although I was now well into the second year of 'pre-clinical' studies I still seemed to be far too squeamish ever to make a doctor.

Unlike many of the other medics, I'd been revolted by dissection, and appalled by having to kill and cut up harmless animals. So how the hell was I going to cope with the blood and guts of real medicine (which, I assumed, would hold no terrors for my tough fellow-students)? To put it mildly, my confidence that I could ever become a doctor was at a pretty low ebb – despite the strong support of my very patient and loving girl-friend.

Then, some time in that second year, an incident occurred which dramatically altered my perspective on 'coping with medicine'.

We were asked to provide volunteers to be the subjects of a research experiment. Lord alone knows what the point of this particular enterprise was supposed to be, but I do remember that it ended up with me strung upside down on some sort of hanging frame in the lab, while a senior lecturer made me breathe in a special way (known to all doctors – because their patients very often do it *accidentally*).

It's called 'over-breathing' – and it lowers the carbon dioxide in your body; the low CO_2 level makes you feel nervous; it also makes your face twitch and your hands go into strange spasms.

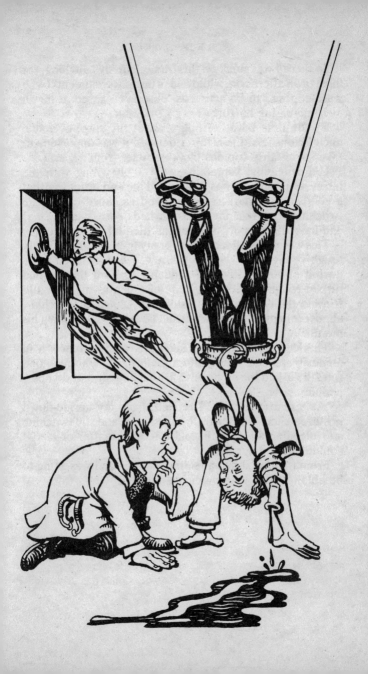

So there I was stuck on this frame, quietly twitching, for most of an afternoon, while one of my fellow-students (who was supposed to be acting as 'observer') gazed at me in ever-increasing horror.

By the time I was getting towards the stage of actual unconsciousness, the lecturer decided it was opportune to take some fairly copious blood samples from my arm.

Unfortunately, something went a bit wrong with the intravenous tube he was using – and the end result was that a good deal of dark, venous blood cascaded out of the twitching arm of the inverted crucified figure (namely, me) and cascaded merrily all over the tiled laboratory floor.

This was really all too much for my friend – an extremely tough young gent who, up till now, I had believed to be devoid of all sensitivity. I suddenly realised that he had turned roughly the same shade of green as the poor old frogs in the next room. He stood up, clutched at a chair, almost collapsed – and then rushed from the lab holding his mouth.

The lecturer had clearly seen this kind of reaction in medical students quite often before. 'D'you feel bad too?' he asked me anxiously. 'Blood and all that do upset people . . .'

'As a matter of fact,' I replied, from my upside-down posture – cheerfully if a trifle indistinctly, and still twitching and bleeding all over the place – 'as a matter of fact, I couldn't give a bugger!'

From then on, I had a feeling that maybe I was going to be able to 'cope with medicine' after all. . . .

4

LIBERACE AND THE ICE-CREAM INTERLUDE

SO, HALF-WAY THROUGH my second year of dissection and physiology, I was at last beginning to get my act together.

But I'd left it very, very late, to put it mildly! So when we got to the second year exams – which you've *got* to pass if you're going to go on to the 'hospital' part of your training, and see real patients – I failed them in glorious style.

(Though not as gloriously as one of my fellow students. Faced with an exam question which read 'Describe the anatomy, blood and nerve supply, structural relations, and embryological development, of the kidney,' he wrote just a single sentence: *'The kidney is kidney-shaped.'* They gave him one per cent.)

One reason why I failed the second year exams was that I'd very unwisely spent a large part of those first two years in court. . . .

You see, Queen's College was located very close to the Old Bailey, and to the local magistrates' court, and to the High Court itself. I found the atmosphere of these places absolutely fascinating.

Indeed, during the two years when I was supposed to be flogging away in the dissecting room or the physiology lab, I'm afraid that all too often I was sitting enthralled in the

33

public gallery at one or other of the courts – listening to the Shirley Bassey Shooting Case, or the Spanish Ambassador Adultery Suit, or the Great Labour Party Drunkenness Libel Action (in which, by the way, the jury were hopelessly wrong: the leaders of the parliamentary Labour Party had clearly been sloshed out of their minds).

Most riveting of all was the wonderful Liberace Case. I spent days in Queen's Bench Court No. 4 watching this – perhaps the most entertaining of all post-war libel actions.

Yes, I *should* have been dissecting poor old Fred, or cutting up a half-dead frog. But by attending the Liberace case across the road, I learned a heck of a lot more about human nature – and particularly about the mysterious subject of homosexuality. (As you can probably imagine, medical students were *never* taught anything about homosexuality. Most of us thought that 'queers' should be locked up in jail – so that they could be cured by the prison MO!)

For the Liberace case hinged around a veiled accusation by an English newspaper that the great showman was gay. Of course, thirty years later we know that he *was* – and that the poor bloke eventually died of AIDS. But in the late fifties, calling somebody a 'poof' was regarded as a most terrible accusation.

The person who had levelled that charge was the *Daily Mirror*'s brilliant but vicious columnist William Connor (known as 'Cassandra'). When Liberace had first arrived in Britain, Cassandra had published a column which read:

He is the summit of sex – the pinnacle of Masculine, Feminine and Neuter. Everything that He, She and It can ever want . . . this deadly, winking, sniggering, snuggling, chromium-plated, scent-impregnated, luminous, quivering, giggling, fruit-flavoured, mincing, ice-cream-covered heap of mother-love . . . reeks with emetic language that can only make grown men long for a quiet corner, an aspidistra, a handkerchief and the old heave-ho. Without doubt, he is the biggest sentimental vomit of all time.

What a nice thing to say about somebody! Not surprisingly, Signor Liberace sued the *Mirror* for libel, and the case arrived in Queen's Bench No. 4 in 1959.

Queen's Bench No. 4 – a splendid Gilbert-and-Sullivan sort of a chamber, with its mellow brown walnut, its green leather Victorian upholstery, its population of gowned and wigged barristers, all presided over by the scarlet-sashed Mr Justice Salmon, sitting under the Royal coat-of-arms. What a contrast with the world of the plaintiff – Wladziu Valentino Liberace, the world's most outrageous pianist (and you had to be pretty careful how you said that).

As I watched for several days, Liberace – wearing a selection from his sixty suits and eighty pairs of shoes – romped through Queen's Bench No. 4, beaming, dimpling, joking, being charming (so much so that one of the lady jurors quite succumbed to him – and even took to exchanging little winks with him).

I was lost in admiration of his brilliant, if heavily toned-down, version of one of his stage or TV performances – but without the help of the piano or the candelabra. (Mr Justice Salmon turned down an application to have the piano brought into court. No application was made on behalf of the candelabra.)

Liberace's case was simple. No, he was not a homosexual – perish the thought! Indeed, these false accusations that he was 'unmanly' had made his poor Mom very ill indeed. . . . With rather greater honesty, he averred that he had been considerably distressed by being described in print as 'the biggest sentimental vomit of all time'.

When Cassandra went into the box, I found that he represented yet another world that fascinated me: the sparky but slightly seedy world of Fleet Street journalism. Cassandra was writing a witty, vitriolic column for the paper with the second biggest circulation on earth – and he clearly *loved* being one of the globe's most famous columnists. But in the witness-box, he slowly began to crumble under the ferocious attack of Mr Gilbert Beyfus,

QC, a very shrewd advocate who the press liked to describe
as 'the Old Fox of the Bar'.

Beyfus had already produced a witness who'd testified
that in private conversation, Cassandra had told her, '*Of
course*, it was libel. We're only defending it because the
Mirror thinks it'll be worth spending £40,000 for a week's
publicity.'

Faced with that accusation, Cassandra could only blus-
ter, 'I think she was a deliberate spy [for Liberace].'

I saw Mr Beyfus rapidly realise that it was possible to
needle Cassandra by such tactics as calling him a 'hack',
and so provoke him into silly, angry answers. At one stage,
he prodded him into irritably denying that his article made
Liberace look ridiculous – an answer that was plainly and
foolishly deceitful.

So, in no time, Beyfus somehow changed the journalist's
image in the jury's minds. For the respected columnist
who'd walked into the witness-box had suddenly been
turned into a bad-tempered elderly man who, over the
years, had launched all sorts of unfair attacks on respected and much-loved British institutions – like Richard
Dimbleby! In some way, Beyfus even managed to suggest
that Cassandra and the *Mirror* were unpatriotic, and
perhaps even against the Royal Family.

It was totally untrue; but Cassandra was never likely to
recover from *that* particular slur! His own counsel – the
cool, brilliant and clear-minded QC Lord Gardiner – did
his best. His final address to the jury was sensible, logical
and unemotional. I listened enraptured as he tried to get
them to look at the actual *words* of Cassandra's article, in
which he'd described Liberace as 'Everything that He, She
and It can ever want'.

Gardiner told the jury, 'It is fantastic to suppose that any
reasonable person reading that sentence would have said
"Oh, I never knew that Mr Liberace went to bed with
men!"'

But Gardiner's logic stood no chance against emotion.

Though the judge's summing-up was full of heavy hints to the jury about the importance of free speech ('Without it, all freedom withers and dies. . . .'), they weren't having any of it!

When I watched them come back into court after considering their verdict, the woman juror who fancied the Great Entertainer took care to wink and smile at him – just to let him know that everything was going to be OK. Inevitably, she and her colleagues awarded Liberace heavy damages (with costs) against the *Mirror* and Cassandra. One quarter of the damages were for the *outrageous* suggestion that the old ivory-tickler was homosexual. Ah well!

Immediately after the case, Liberace announced that he was 'delighted that his reputation had been vindicated by a British jury' – and gave the jurywoman his autograph. And I returned to the dissecting room across the road, having missed about a week of carving up old Fred.

*   *   *

So really, you can see why I failed the second year exams!

Thank heavens, we were allowed one more shot at them about three months later. If you failed on *that* occasion, you were out on your ear, and had to seek another career.

Some of the lads who were chucked out used their medical knowledge to become drug sales reps, which was very sensible of them. My plan – in the event of a second failure – was to make a career as a contestant in TV quiz games, which was obviously complete insanity.

The rationale for this dotty idea was that I'd already had a brief frolic on a television general knowledge game called *Criss-Cross Quiz* – showing off on TV was clearly going to be part of the pattern of my life – and I'd been quite intoxicated by the experience.

I loved the TV studios (Granada's, at Manchester) and the way that the tatty sets could be made to appear glamorous and exciting on the screen. Even the machine-like sliding-door through which the contestants stepped out on to the floor turned out to be opened and closed by a sweaty, crouching stage-hand, rather than by remote control (as it seemed to the TV viewer).

It was just like appearing in an amiable down-at-heel old theatre which had been rather desperately tarted-up to impress the punters. (And I must say that, even today, most television studios haven't changed much!)

I only won ten quid on the quiz show, but I was already seduced by the mystique of TV broadcasting. Frankly, I was also rather seduced by the false glitz (as opposed to the *real* glitz) of being met at Manchester station by a studio car – and being sent home after the show *in a first-class sleeper*. Wow!

The British Rail sleeper seemed to me to have wonderful overtones of the Orient Express – especially when (half an hour out of romantic Manchester) the connecting door of the next compartment opened: there stood a tall, willowy brunette lady in her undies.

After I'd blinked, I realised that this was one of the other contestants in the quiz game. 'Sorry,' she said. 'I thought I was opening a cupboard.'

Slightly unbelievably, she came in and sat down on my bunk. Whisky appeared from somewhere, and in rather stilted fashion we spent forty-five minutes or so discussing how we'd got on in the TV quiz.

I must have been staggeringly naive, because it never occurred to me that she had any intention of having her wicked way with me. Not that she stood a chance: for a start, I had a lovely girl-friend waiting for me at home. And anyway, the willowy brunette – attractive as she was – was far, far too elderly for me. She must have been all of thirty-five, poor old soul. . . .

So, eventually she went back – still chaste – to her compartment. But the heady excitement of this encounter set my head dancing to the rhythm of the wheels. Obviously, a life in TV would be like this *all* the time!

As I say, I'd done abysmally at the quiz game, and only

came away with £10 in Premium Bonds. But the experience did give me the mad taste for television – and it was doubtless as a result of it that I ended up having quite an entertaining run on *Mastermind* some twenty years later.

Anyway – thank heavens, I soon gave up the crazy idea of making a living as a TV quiz contestant, and settled down to studying hard for a change. With the help of luck and a following breeze, I passed the second year exam at the end of the summer.

So I realised with an enormous sense of relief that after a *very* shaky start my medical career was now more or less on course. I could at last leave behind me the ghastly dissection room and physiology lab of Queen's College.

In October 1959, I'd be starting at its associated hospital – Queen's Cottage Hospital – which was located some miles away in a London suburb. I knew that the atmosphere there was totally different (in more ways than one – for the smell was a good deal nicer). And, best of all, the patients would be (mostly) alive instead of dead. The world was looking better.

In the meantime, I could relax and look forward to several months of vacation – during what turned out to be the glorious late summer of 1959. I needed money to keep myself going, and by some fluke I chose exactly the right job for that super summer: selling ice-cream from a bicycle.

*   *   *

In a way, selling ice-cream was a bit like being a junior doctor. My colleagues of the choc-ice and I wore medical-style white coats; we worked strange, long hours; we did our best to keep the public happy; we put in an awful lot of legwork; and we hardly ever got any proper meals. (But, as I discovered when I eventually became a junior doctor, you earn three times as much by selling ice-cream. . . .)

My boss for that summer – and my mentor in the gentle art of flogging *gelati* – was a person of repulsive aspect, who went by the name of Bert.

Bert's 'operation room' was a seedy basement in North London, jam-packed with fridges and bikes. On the front of every bike was a formidably heavy ice-box. Each day, about fifteen of us lads turned up in our white coats and filled the ice-boxes with lollies, chocs and cornets (plus a great steaming lump of solid carbon dioxide – dry ice – to keep things cold). Then we'd pedal off to our various 'stations', sell the lot – on commission – as fast as possible, and cycle back for more.

The appalling Bert – who was making a packet out of us – despised all his regular salesmen, and openly referred to them as 'dirt' when talking to me. Why he did this I don't know, but I suppose he reckoned that, as a doctor-to-be, I was somehow worthy of his confidence. Also, he felt he had a kind of affinity with medicine, as I was shortly to discover.

One day when trade was slack, he took me aside and proudly told me his life history. He claimed that he'd started out working in fairs and markets as a sideshow barker, but had soon graduated to running his own stall. He said – and from the way he did the patter I think it may have been true – that his great forte had been selling a patent medicine – Dr Hextable-Smith's Cure-All.

Of course, in those days, Bert used to represent himself to the public as Dr Hextable-Smith in person. He told me with nostalgia of how he would appear at the stall dressed in a black frock-coat, with a stethoscope dangling from his neck, and a pocket watch on a brass chain.

'Ladies and gentlemen,' he'd cry. 'You all know my name and why I am reduced to appearing before you like this. Once I was in Harley Street but then in a moment of misplaced compassion, I tried to help a young girl in trouble. Struck orf by the BMA I was – and left with no way of earning my living except to sell this wonderful medicine, my own invention, which cures arthritis, baldness, dandruff, warts, heart disease, chest trouble, stones, afflictions of the liver, nervous ailments, and difficulties with the personal parts. . . .'

The crowd would listen to this, open-mouthed, except for one large Welshman with a walking-stick who would stand at the back guffawing and jeering. When Bert had finished, the Welshman would limp forward and shout aggressively, 'All right then, doctor-boyo. Let's see if your concoction can cure my rheumatism, that is the despair of every medical man in Wales.'

Bert would proffer him a bottle of Dr Hextable-Smith's Cure-All, and the Welshman would take a deep swig of it. Then he'd suddenly start back as if electrified, and fling his walking-stick in the air, shouting, 'It works! It works! The pain has gone at last.'

Finally, he'd caper off madly across the fairground bellowing snatches from Welsh hymns, while the crowd fought each other for the privilege of handing their pound notes over to Dr Hextable-Smith – sorry, I mean Bert.

Bert's medical career had gone very well for a number of years, until the large Welshman and he had a falling-out over how the money should be divided. The result of this little disagreement between colleagues was that Bert finished up in Bart's Hospital, with ten teeth missing, three cracked ribs, and a dislocated elbow. He told me he didn't find Dr Hextable-Smith's Cure-All a lot of help in the post-operative period. . . .

So, Bert had turned to the ice-cream game instead – and turned to it with astonishing success. I eventually discovered that despite the scruffy appearance of the premises he worked from, Bert had grown rich enough on ice-cream to be able to spend part of every winter cruising in the Caribbean!

He seemed to have achieved his success by totally disregarding all the normal rules of society. (If he'd been a real doctor, he'd probably have risen right to the top of the profession.) He thought that everyone he came into contact with could be ignored, bribed, or bullied, and – sad to say – he was very often right.

If a man from the ice-cream wholesaler arrived with

awkward questions, a few five pound notes changed hands, and that was that. If somebody from the ministry of this-or-that came along, demanding to know why regulations weren't being observed, Bert would blithely explain that he 'couldn't read, mate' and show the official the door. If rival ice-cream men poached on our territory, Bert's remedy was simple. Curling his lip into a ferocious snarl he would hiss, 'Gerrahtovit – or I'll run yer down.'

It was a brave man who failed to heed his warning.

Fights between Bert's lads and the boys from rival firms of Brawl's or Elcascara ice-cream were common, especially when our leader decided to 'pirate' at a football match or race meeting where one of the other companies had already paid hundreds of pounds for the ice-cream concession. In we'd go through the gates in a van, white jackets and ice-boxes hidden under our coats; once we were among the crowd, it was covers off and every man selling for all he was worth! Eventually, of course, the Brawl's ice-cream men would discover us and all hell would break loose, with fists flying and most people except Bert (who prudently carried an iron bar for protection) coming off a trifle contused.

Even out in the streets, conflicts between ice-cream men were frequent. On one memorable occasion, six of Bert's boys were cavalry-charged by the bicycle troops of the Elcascara company in the middle of the local High Street. I remember one of our chaps – a weedy, decrepit individual with a long red nose – staggering back to base afterwards with his glasses smashed, his white jacket torn, his hair awry, his trousers covered in ice-cream (it makes a lovely weapon in a fight), and his nostrils pouring blood.

'Good job I know a bit of judo,' he gasped through swollen lips. 'I did the ol' stomach throw on three or four of 'em, and that soon settled *their* hash.'

I tried not to get too involved in the ice-cream wars myself, though for a brief period I was in serious dispute with a rival who thought I was trying to take over his 'patch'

– an enormous and lucrative block of flats where the population lived largely on choc-ices and fish and chips.

One Saturday lunch-time, to the delight of dozens of applauding children, we had an eyeball-to-eyeball confrontation, complete with corny dialogue ('I'll kill yer, if you don't leave my flats alone, you bleedin' medical stoodent'; 'Take your hand off my white coat, Squire, before I smash your bloody teeth in', etc, etc).

That particular clash ended when we discovered that the kids had not only stolen a good deal of our ice-cream, but a good deal of our day's takings as well – and had let down my enemy's tyres into the bargain (which I thought was very decent of them).

I had no further trouble with this chap, because the following week the police discovered that he was in fact the Phantom Flasher of the local mating grounds – a lad who was in the habit of gaily exposing himself to all and sundry and then pedalling off on his ice-cream cart at top speed, leaving the irate (or envious) lovers waving their fists behind him. The cops happily nicked him – thereby removing my competition.

Several of the other stop-me-and-buy-one lads who I came across were also a trifle bizarre. One of Bert's boys, for instance, suddenly developed what I can only term an acute ice-cream phobia (? gelatophobia). He found that he really hated the stuff and became extremely agitated whenever he was in the same room with it.

For a week or so, he couldn't go out on his round at all but eventually Bert blackmailed him into it somehow. Six hours later, he still hadn't come back. The ice-cream boys went round to his house and found him sitting happily on his bike on the living-room floor, gazing at the walls, curtains and ceilings which were dripping with ice-cream. He'd taken twenty pounds worth of the hated stuff home, and then had a simply splendid time hurling it at the walls just as hard as he could.

The funny thing was that this violent outburst seemed to

have cured his problem and he was quite happy to work with choc-ices, lollies and cornets once more. I couldn't help feeling that this technique sounded like a useful 'alternative' way of treating phobias!

Yet another of Bert's minions grew somewhat disenchanted with the ice-cream business one day and simply took off on his bicycle down the Great West Road, carrying some ten pounds' worth of the stuff in front of him. I think a police car eventually caught up with him somewhere near Reading. Incidentally, this type of 'fugue' (to use what I believe is the approved psychiatric term for a hysterical flight) forms quite a common syndrome in the trade, so much so that Bert told me that there's even a standard term ('flyers') for ice-cream men who go walkabout in this fashion.

Still, I found the stop-me-and-buy-one business not so bad, even if every now and then I did lose a couple of pounds' worth of ice-cream by falling off my bike and into the road – an immediate signal to the local children to pounce on such of the goodies as had not been flattened by passing cars. The open air life and exercise were healthy and I felt amazingly fit by the time I was ready to start at Queen's Cottage Hospital at the end of the summer.

A few months later, I was working in the out-patients department of the hospital. One morning I was told to examine a small boy to whom I used to sell ice-cream in 'my' block of flats.

We recognised each other immediately (doubtless I looked the same in the white coat), but he seemed somewhat puzzled as to the reason for my presence in the hospital.

Eventually he managed to find a solution.

'Did you,' he said to me with big eyes, 'did you get the sack from the ice-cream job and take up doctoring instead?'

5

REAL LIVE PATIENTS

STARTING AT THE hospital was like seeing the dawn coming up – at long last, I found I was actually happy in my work.

The hospital seemed to be on a different planet from the cold, laboratory world of the pre-clinical college. The main reason for this, I need hardly say, was that Queen's Cottage Hospital had real *live* patients! It was enormously satisfying just to sit down and talk with them, to listen to their problems – and, of course, to try and work out some sort of diagnosis (usually mistaken in my case, I might add) of the symptoms that had brought them in.

However, for the first twelve weeks of our three-year stint at the hospital, the authorities very sensibly didn't let us actually *do* anything to patients, like stitching them up, or sticking needles in them. (After all, the only thing we were qualified for was carving them up into little pieces after they were dead.)

So, instead, we were sent on a very valuable three-month 'Introductory Course', which was intended to teach us two vital things:

(a) how to interview patients;

(b) how to examine them.

You'll note that I *don't* say 'How to communicate with them.' I'm sorry to add that learning communication

45

was never a strong point at this or any other medical school.

And I'm afraid things haven't changed much over the years since then. Shortly before I finished writing this book, a conference organised by the World Federation for Medical Education was told that medical students *still* receive almost no guidance on how to talk to patients, or how to break bad news.

As a result, researchers have come across such recent incidents as these:

A surgeon was told by a forty-year-old patient that she'd prefer not to lose her breast. He replied, 'There's not much there worth keeping, is there?'

A junior hospital doctor found a man crying because he was dying of cancer. He told him unsympathetically, 'Well, we *all* have to die some time.'

A woman whose daughter had been diagnosed by a specialist as having a brain tumour asked the eminent consultant to tell her how much improvement could be expected. He replied, 'About as much as you'd expect from a pet dog.'

Why in heaven's name do so many doctors (very far from all, of course) go on like this?

I think it's because of their disastrous training, which neglects communication almost totally. Indeed, good though our introductory course was, it kicked off on the first day with a staggering example (provided by the man who was the uncrowned king of the hospital) of how to make a complete and utter cock-up of communication.

For we were given a *most* unfortunate preliminary pep talk by the hospital's famous senior surgeon, who told the students just two things which were supposed to prepare us for dealing with patients:

(a) that we were not to laugh at the ignorant working classes because they liked football instead of rugger;

(b) that we must steel ourselves to put up with examining coloured people!

At this point, he noticed that a friend of mine in the front row of the lecture theatre was decidedly *black*.

For some incredible reason, the senior surgeon tried to get himself out of this extremely awkward situation by publicly questioning my friend as to his religion (which was Christian) – a move which merely increased the general fog of embarrassment pervading the lecture room.

I'm afraid I began to get a distinct feeling that consultant surgeons were not necessarily either free of prejudice or blessed with great tact.

After this appalling start, the introductory course improved no end. We had lectures from the hospital pharmacist on how to put the secret symbol 'R' – an invocation to the Egyptian god Horus – at the start of a prescription ('Two heads are better than one, gentlemen!').

We had lectures on the supreme importance of medical confidentiality – learning that never, *ever* did you disclose in casual conversation the secrets which a patient entrusted you with. And we were warned what to do if someone asked us to do an illegal abortion: at all costs, say 'No!'

But mainly, we learned how to examine patients; and how to interview them.

Examination of a patient isn't easy, and it can take years to learn how to feel things under the skin, and how to interpret the strange gurgles and clicks which you hear down a stethoscope. Unfortunately, in the early weeks you have to do your examining *en masse* – in other words, you may get twenty seconds to listen to a patient's heart before it's time for the next bloke to have a go!

Most days, we invaded the wards and the out-patient department in large groups of twelve or fifteen at a time, flaunting our newly-purchased 'tubes' and throat-torches, taking our turn at examining patients' chests and bellies and eyes and tonsils – and frequently being totally confused about what it was we were supposed to be looking for.

Frankly, I was quite amazed at the way in which the

long-suffering (and usually *very* long-waiting) patients put up with all this! Most of them seemed to be touchingly grateful that anyone showed any interest in them at all – even if we were only a bunch of twenty-year-old students. In fact, many of them mistakenly thought that we were 'the young doctors' – and indeed we were told by some of our seniors (quite wrongly in my view) to say to patients that we were 'doctors in training'.

This deception was very stupid, really – because I reckoned then, and I reckon now, that the vast majority of people didn't at all mind being examined by medical students, *provided* that somebody explained what the heck was going on.

Alas, that wasn't always the case. One image of the early days of the introductory course is still in my mind's eye: a poor bloke was lying peacefully in his hospital bed, when a rugby team of young medics – who'd been detailed to listen to his chest – suddenly pounced on him.

He started to say 'What actually is the purpose of all this . . .' But before he could really finish the question, several lusty lads had hauled him upright and whipped up his pyjama jacket at the back – and at least half a dozen stethoscopes were already plonked on his shoulder-blades.

No wonder the poor chap was alarmed, because, as far as I recall, there was nothing wrong with his chest at all: he'd come in to be investigated for an ulcer.

This was clearly no way to treat a human being. Yet let me say very firmly that by the standards of those days, Queen's Cottage Hospital was actually one of the most enlightened of institutions; I'm virtually certain that patients' rights were disregarded far more flagrantly at some other more traditionally-minded hospitals.

For instance, my friend Dr Richard Gordon tells me that at *his* teaching hospital (St Fanny's-in-the-East) some years earlier, the general idea was that when a patient was admitted to the wards, her illness immediately ceased to be her 'property' – and became instead the property of the

consultant in charge of her case. Therefore, what happened to her in the way of diagnosis and treatment while she was in hospital *was simply no business of hers* – and none of the staff would dream of discussing such matters with her!

At our hospital in 1959, they certainly didn't take so extreme a view. Nonetheless, it would have been almost unthinkable for a patient to say 'Pardon me, doc – but I'd like to discuss this with you before you start cutting lumps out of me!' I'm afraid we rapidly learned the lesson that patients were not encouraged to ask questions.

Anyway, during those three months on the introductory course, we gradually learned the basics of listening to lungs and hearts, and also of palpating abdomens, loins and groins. By the end of that time, I felt *almost* sure that I could diagnose a hernia.

Well, very nearly. . . .

*   *   *

We also began to learn how to go about the all-important business of 'taking a history'.

What this time-honoured phrase means is *interviewing the patient*, to find out exactly what his or her symptoms are.

Now that may seem simple to you. In fact, it's an extremely difficult business, for two reasons:

Firstly, very few men or women have the innate ability to talk to a person and to draw out a coherent story from them – that's why good TV interviewers are in such short supply.

Secondly, most people (and therefore most patients) find great difficulty in expressing themselves clearly and succinctly, without wittering off down side-avenues (and *that's* why most TV interviews are heavily edited).

You probably find it difficult to accept what I've just said. But again and again on that introductory course, pairs of us medical students would be given (say) half an hour to interview a patient and then report back on his or her symptoms. And again and again, at the end of the half-hour, the two students would return having got absolutely *nowhere*.

The combination of our own ignorance of interviewing skills plus the difficulty which many of the patients had in talking to us led to results which were often quite ludicrous.

For instance, this is the kind of dialogue in which many of us found ourselves involved:

1ST STUDENT:	Good-morning, Mr Jones. What's wrong with you?
PATIENT:	That's what I came here to find out, isn't it?
2ND STUDENT:	No, no, sir. What brought you here?
PATIENT:	I came on a number 13 bus.
1ST STUDENT:	No, Mr Jones – we want to know *why* you've come to the hospital?
PATIENT:	To be cured of course, young man.
2ND STUDENT:	Yes, but what seems to be the trouble?
PATIENT:	There's no question of '*seems* to' about it! I hope you're not suggesting I'm making all this up.
1ST STUDENT:	Making all *what* up? What are you actually complaining of?
PATIENT:	Oh, I'm not *complaining*, doctor! No, I've never been one to complain. Even when I was in the Catering Corps in Korea in '51, I never, ever complained. Tough time we had out there too – did you ever hear about the Korean war, doctor?
CONSULTANT (*entering stage left*):	Well now, lads – what's your diagnosis of Mr Jones?

1ST STUDENT: Er . . . I'm afraid we haven't found
                out what his symptoms are yet, sir.
PATIENT: My symptoms? Well, why didn't you
                ask me?

I'm afraid one or two of us students never really learned to
'take a history' at all. Towards the end of the introductory
course, a Welsh friend of mine spent perhaps thirty minutes
interviewing a man, and was then required to make his
'presentation' to the consultant and to the rest of the
students.

He began by saying *in front of the patient*, 'I haven't
really been able to get much out of this man, sir, because
he's not very intelligent.' The effect on the patient was, of
course, quite horrendous.

Very wisely, that boy eventually became a pathologist.
All his patients are dead, so I suppose they don't take much
offence at his remarks.

*   *   *

Actually, this particular bloke did once treat a live patient
in recent years. While on a seaside holiday, he saw a girl
drowning, rescued her, gave her the 'kiss of life' – and
finally handed her over to the ambulancemen. Then, as he
wandered off up the beach, he saw a man coming to
intercept him.

'Excuse me!' the chap cried.

My friend thought 'It's a press man! He's going to
interview me!'

Delusions of national fame danced in his head. ('The
Quiet Hero . . . The Gallant Doctor Who Tried To Walk
Away Without Giving His Name . . .')

'Yes?' he said, turning to the man.

''Scuse me – didn't you use to play scrum-half for Cardiff
second team?'

*   *   *

I've said a few pages back that 'taking a history' means interviewing a patient – but not necessarily (alas) communicating with him.

All doctors are trained in this curious business of 'taking a history'; once you've learned it, it's a very efficient way of ferreting out facts. Unfortunately, it may not be so much fun when you're on the receiving end of it. Let me explain.

We were taught to ask certain questions in a rather rigid, structured way – and not to let the patient stray away from the interrogatory path on which we were leading him, even if this meant repeating a question again and again.

The classic example of this is the 'How long have you had the pain?' saga:

CONSULTANT: What's the trouble, Mrs Harris?

MRS HARRIS: This pain in my tummy, doctor, like a knife it is, and –

CONSULTANT (*interrupting her*): How long have you had the pain?

MRS HARRIS: Terrible at times, it is; and some nights I find –

CONSULTANT (*interrupting again*): How long have you had the pain?

MRS HARRIS: My Bill said to me, 'Vera,' he said –

CONSULTANT (*cutting in again*): How long have you had the pain?

MRS HARRIS: Of course, I find aspirin does help it sometimes, but –

CONSULTANT (*bitingly*): How *long* have you had the pain?

MRS HARRIS: Eh? Oh, quite a while, doctor.

CONSULTANT (*scathingly*): And how long is 'quite a while'?

Repetitions like this could go on for three or four minutes – at the end of which the consultant would at last be able to write in his notes 'Pain for six months' – and then move on to exacting a precise answer to his *next* question.

Pretty brutal stuff, eh?

In fact, I must admit this rigid system of questioning does work very well with most patients, and does often save a lot of time. For instance, with a co-operative and quick-witted patient, the above conversation would have proceeded very briskly and efficiently, like this:

CONSULTANT: What's the trouble, Mrs Jones?
MRS JONES: Pain in the tummy, doctor – just here.
CONSULTANT: How long have you had it?
MRS JONES: About six months, doctor.
CONSULTANT: What time of day d'you get it?
MRS JONES: About two hours after meals – and it wakes me up about 2 a.m.
CONSULTANT: Does anything help it?
MRS JONES: Food, doctor; antacids – and milk.

That little episode of 'history taking' would take no more than twenty-five seconds – yet by this time, the doctor would already be fairly certain that this woman has either a duodenal or gastric ulcer.

So the traditional, rigid way of 'taking a history' *can* be pretty efficient.

However, it is of course absolutely useless to stick to it if a patient wants to break out of the rigid structure and talk about his or her fears or emotions. *That*, alas, was not encouraged. . . .

*   *   *

Because I enjoyed listening to people (and also writing things down) I rapidly convinced myself that I was good at taking and presenting a history. Sad to say, this was not entirely true.

For instance, somewhere about the end of the introductory course, I was sent to interview and examine a woman of about fifty. I got on well with her, and quickly established in my own mind that her symptoms and clinical signs indicated that she was suffering from malignant deposits inside her chest – secondary to a breast cancer which had been removed some years previously.

So, when the consultant eventually arrived at the bedside to interrogate me, I proudly produced my little 'presentation' – making it absolutely clear that the signs which I'd found in her chest were related to the breast cancer in the past.

As I smugly finished what I thought had been rather a neat piece of succinct reportage, I looked at the woman – and realised with utter horror that, until now, she had had no idea whatever that her present 'chest trouble' was connected to the breast tumour. She'd assumed that it had been cured years ago.

'You realise what you've done?' said one of the other students to me *sotto voce*. 'You might as well have said "Thank you, madam – and good-night". . . .'

It was true. I had publicly given this poor woman her own death sentence. It was clear that – no matter how much I'd enjoyed the introductory course and my dealings with patients – I still had a very, very great deal to learn about people.

6

ON THE MEDICAL FIRM

The introductory course had been rather like a wonderful game – a game in which we'd been able to 'play doctors' for the first time, but without any responsibilities whatever. But now life was beginning to get distinctly more serious.

I began to realise this the day on which I entered the hospital's post-mortem room: a grim place in which each day the pathologists showed us what had caused the deaths of the various patients who'd expired in the hospital (or else been brought in dead) during the previous twenty-four hours.

That morning, I'd picked up a tabloid newspaper and read its horrific lead story:

PARENTS AND THREE CHILDREN DIE IN FIRE

Naturally, it didn't occur to me that the tragedy – which had occurred in some overcrowded London home – had anything to do with *me*.

But when my friends and I jostled cheerfully into the PM room, I suddenly found the newspaper story made flesh – charred flesh – in front of me. On the great cold white slab were five human windpipes (two large and three pathetically small), filled with the black muck which death by fire causes.

The pathologist succinctly explained to us that, as is usual in fire disasters, the family had been quickly choked

56

to death by the instant and devastating effect of the hot smoke which they'd inhaled into their windpipes. He also made the point that rapid extinction in this way was at any rate preferable to being slowly and agonizingly incinerated alive by the flames. He added that the instantaneous lethal effect of fumes had spared St Joan of Arc and many another martyr from more than a few seconds of pain.

For once, even the most irreverent of the medical students were briefly (well, *very* briefly) quiet and thoughtful as we made our way out of the PM room, and adjourned to the refectory for an uneasy lunch of Spam fritters.

We were soon to be exposed to tragedy and death on the wards, too – for we had to come to terms quite rapidly with the fact that some of the in-patients who were now allotted to each of us were, quite simply, not going to make it. Depressingly often, one came into the ward in the morning and found an empty bed where yesterday's patient had been.

I remember particularly Mr Davis: a nice, plump man of about forty who'd just had a coronary. He was funny, lively and cheerful, and he reminded me of my girl-friend's dad. I went in each day, chatted to him and examined him – and I hadn't the least doubt that a bloke who was such *fun* (despite being forced to lie flat on his back for six weeks – which was the treatment for coronaries at that time) would soon be fit and well again.

But one morning I wandered into the ward, and the sheets on his empty bed were crisp and new. In the middle of the night, that nice, jolly man had clutched his chest and died. I'm now rather doubtful whether the treatment he was having was right. As I've just said, *all* coronary – 'heart attack' – patients were kept lying absolutely flat (no raising the head allowed!) for six weeks. They were also given a derivative of rat poison to try and prevent the blood from clotting.

All this, it was firmly believed, was the best possible therapy – and woe betide a coronary patient who tried to sit up! As far as I remember, they even had to get on the bedpan lying down.

Within a surprisingly short period of years, this entire fashion of treatment had completely gone – today, 'coronaries' are mobilized as quickly as possible. One reason for this is that it's realised that keeping any patient in bed for several weeks exposes him to the major risk of getting clots in his leg veins. These clots can then travel to his lungs and kill him. That, I suspect, may well have happened to poor Mr Davis.

*   *   *

I pointed out to Mike Beall, one of my closest student friends who later became a consultant at the Mayo Clinic, that fashions in medicine did seem to swing rather violently, didn't they?

After all, all of us students had laughed heartily at the *ridiculous* medical treatments of previous generations (like whipping out the whole of the large intestine to 'cure' people who were supposed to be suffering from some sort of 'bowel poisoning' – the results were disastrous).

Wasn't it possible, I asked him, that some of the treatments we were being taught *now* in 1960 were just as wrong? Although Mike was far and away the most brilliant student of his year, he just couldn't see this at all. Modern medicine was now *scientific* – so that was it.

Nearly all the students – being mostly of a conservative disposition – took the same view. What our consultants taught us was *right*. When you went on the wards, you simply accepted what they said. Only the very bold would argue. Because if you argued, you could be risking your chances of a future job.

*   *   *

Now you may wonder what on earth us ignorant load of pea-brained juveniles could have *done* for any sick person on the wards at this early stage of our careers. (After all, none of us even knew how to put on a Band-Aid.)

Well, we did carry out most of the basic tests on their

blood, urine and bowel motions: this was part of our jobs as general 'ward dogsbodies'. And occasionally (not often), we picked up signs or symptoms which the qualified doctors had missed.

But I honestly think that the main thing we were able to give the patients was a bit of companionship and friendliness. I have to admit that, in these early days, we certainly knew next to nothing about their diseases, half of which we couldn't even pronounce.

The patients, however, did a lot for *us* by letting us examine them endlessly.

By now, we'd learned the full routine of examining a patient (even if we couldn't yet do it very well), working slowly and systematically through his central nervous system, his cardiovascular system, his respiratory system, and so on – tickling the soles of his feet (to test his reflexes), hitting his knees with little hammers (ditto), and tapping his chest with one middle finger on the other in the odd way doctors have (the combined sound and feeling give you some idea of what things are like underneath the skin – it's analogous to tapping a hollow wall for the secret panel).

On a good day, I'd have gone over a dozen or so patients, putting all of them through this long, thorough routine, hoping – as each of us did – to find some unusual and interesting 'clinical sign' which might bring glory when demonstrated to a consultant!

This whole painstaking process of giving a patient a complete 'overhaul' will pick up most medical disorders – but it takes the best part of half an hour to do. Little did we realise that most of us would one day be ending up in a working environment (the NHS GP's surgery) which more or less demands that you see one patient *every five minutes*!

*　　　*　　　*

I was now on the very lowest rung of what's called the 'Medical Firm'. *Medical*, you'll notice – as opposed to *surgical*.

In case you're not quite clear about the distinction between 'medical' and 'surgical', it's this:

Medicine (often referred to as 'general medicine' or – if you're American – 'internal medicine') is the speciality which is concerned with diseases of the heart, lungs, liver, stomach, thyroid and so on – diseases *which can usually be treated by drugs or other non-surgical measures*. It's generally considered by its practitioners to be a good deal more intellectual and brain-taxing than surgery!

Surgery is much more concerned with purely *structural* abnormalities of the body, which can be put right by operation. I mean mundane defects like hernias and varicose veins, as well as life-threatening ones such as intestinal obstruction, bowel cancer or bleeding stomach ulcers.

The consultants in medicine tended to regard the consultants in surgery as 'plumbers' or 'technicians', which was a trifle unfair, to say the least.

But it *was* quite obvious that the personalities of the two groups differed very greatly. Medical consultants (who like to be known as 'physicians') were, as they are today, generally rather more introverted and thoughtful men. (And at that time they *were* nearly all men; female consultants were rare.)

Physicians take great pleasure in carrying out very careful examination and investigation of patients before committing themselves to a diagnosis, let alone coming to any decision as to what to do. A patient with a complex disease holds all the challenge of a really tough crossword for them.

In contrast, the surgeons were generally far more ebullient and extrovert. Risk-takers by nature, they were the sort of men who delight in overtaking in fast cars – preferably very *expensive* fast cars. Their exchanges with patients tended to be a trifle one-sided: a quick elucidation of symptoms, a brief examination, and then 'We'll take that out for you next Tuesday; goodbye.'

When I'm writing one of my 'agony columns' these days,

and I print the words 'Do talk this over carefully with your surgeon before agreeing to have your breast removed,' I can't help remembering those men.

Most (not all) of them would never have *dreamed* of 'talking things over' with a patient – at least not an NHS one. Some of today's surgeons are different and more approachable – but others, alas, still think they're super-men.

Such immense self-confidence is fine in the operating theatre, but not so good when a patient desperately needs reassurance about losing the bit of him that you're going to lop off.

*   *   *

So by now we'd all been assigned to either a Medical or a Surgical 'Firm' – in my case a medical one – on which we'd have responsibility for some of the firm's patients.

I should explain that in a British teaching hospital, a 'firm' is a unit, led by a consultant (that is, a specialist), who is the boss of a hierarchy which looks roughly like the table opposite.

One important point to make about this table is that the vast majority of the actual work is done by the unfortunate house officer – who at that time was working far in excess of 100 hours a week. (It's only slightly less today.) In contrast, a few of the consultants worked only a dozen hours a week or less in the hospital – just turning up for a couple of clinics and ward rounds.

One or two consultants still followed the old god-like habit of having their entire firm lined up to greet them on the mornings when they arrived at the hospital door – ideally by Rolls-Royce.

As they entered the portals, their troops would fall behind and escort them up the stairs to the ward – where sister would welcome them, and a splendid retinue of nurses would join the procession around the beds – a

Consultant (age 40–65, and either rich or fairly well off)

Senior Registrar (age 35–40, and not well off)

Registrar (age 27–35, and quite poor)

House Officer (age 23–26, and *very* poor!)

8–12 Medical Students (age 20–21, and mostly broke)

procession which was known as a 'ward round' or 'grand round'. No wonder the patients were impressed. . . .

If a consultant had (say) fifty patients on his wards, then each of us students would be responsible for about four or five of them, and would be expected to know everything about them, to help at any procedures they had to undergo, and (if things didn't work out too well) to attend their post-mortems.

In addition to the ward work, the students would attend the consultant's out-patient clinics, and take turns to examine his patients there as well.

As I say, my first assignment was six months to a Medical Firm, led by an elderly and famous consultant, who I'll call Dr Robert Morecambe. To us, he seemed nice, but very old indeed, for he told us he could remember examining cases of pneumonia in the Spanish 'flu epidemic of 1918.

His staff treated him like a minor deity and told us in hushed tones that he was 'a marvellous clinician' – an expression which meant that he was outstandingly good at making a diagnosis from the history and examination alone (rather than lots of scientific tests). Dr Morecambe rather reinforced that point on his first ward round with us, when he spent some time in explaining to us that British doctors were 'far better than American doctors as clinicians.'

He then demonstrated his famed clinical skills on a patient with a suspected effusion of fluid in the chest, using finger-tapping and his stethoscope to find it – and made jovial fun of those who thought the fluid was on the left side rather than on the right (personally, I hadn't a clue).

We were terrifically impressed by all this – at least until the patient's X-rays came back the following day. The fluid was actually on the *left* side – so he'd been totally mistaken. I don't think Dr Morecambe's registrars ever told him he'd got it completely the wrong way round: after all, he was nearing the end of his long and very distinguished career. And their future job prospects were to a great extent in his hands.

The other thing that struck me very forcibly about him was this: when patients walked into his out-patient clinic, *he never got up from his chair*.

This simple omission hit me like a blow in the face. On our first morning with him in the out-patient department, he was sitting at his desk, flanked by eight or ten of us. The door opened, and in walked a woman patient. To me (and quite a few of the others) what we had to do was clear: we were programmed by our parents and schools with the phrase 'When a lady walks into a room, you stand up.'

Alas, Dr Morecambe made it quite clear that this was not a 'lady' – this was a patient. And you did not get up from your chair for mere patients. . . . At least, not NHS patients.

Since many (not all) of the other consultants appeared to take exactly the same attitude, I'm afraid we all learned the lesson rather rapidly. I'm ashamed to say that it was many years later before I finally grasped that *whoever* comes into your consulting room – be it Royal or rat-catcher – the least you can do is stand up and try and make him or her feel welcome.

Alas, some doctors still haven't realised this fact, which is why when their patients walk in, they sit looking down at their desks – sometimes already writing out the prescription, I'm afraid.

*   *   *

But we spent much more time on the wards themselves, rather than learning consultation manners (or, perhaps, lack of them) in the out-patients department.

In the men's and women's medical wards, four or five in-patients were assigned to me. What I had to do was to see them as soon as possible after they were admitted, take a full history, examine them thoroughly from top to toe, and write it all up in the notes.

A couple of my first batch of in-patients were adult women (one had thyroid trouble and one, I think, had diabetes) – and you may wonder how on earth a callow male medical student coped with asking a woman to strip off so that he could spend half an hour or so examining her body.

The answer, surprisingly enough, was that it was quite easy and free of problems. I was extremely fortunate in that I felt very little embarrassment in being alone with a naked patient. Well, *almost* alone: we were supposed to ask a nurse to chaperone us, but the girls were so hard-worked that this wasn't often possible.

So because most male doctors are (perhaps understandably) frightened of being accused of sexual assault on female patients, we were taught to employ an alternative technique of protecting ourselves whilst examining women: leave the curtains open so that passing nursing staff could see in. (That's why so many doctors have the similar habit – when they do intimate examinations – of leaving the consulting-room doors open.)

You may also feel inclined to ask the rather personal question 'Weren't you sexually excited by these naked female bodies?'

And I shall be delighted to tell you the answer – which is 'No'!

I don't know why, but I think that like most doctors I've been lucky enough to be able to completely divorce what I've seen in the ward or the clinic from my own sexual feelings. Patients are patients – not sex-objects.

I've noticed that people who are very puritanical about sex – like journalists who work on the newspapers that feature nudes – often find this particular fact extremely difficult to believe. But it's true: to be quite frank, I have never in my life experienced an erection at the sight of a stripped-off patient, no matter how attractive. I think that the same is true of most male doctors: certainly, none of my personal friends in medicine has *ever* said to me anything like 'Have you seen the fantastic boobs on the bird in bed number three?' – though soon after I qualified, I did have a rather repellent colleague who insisted on doing vaginal examinations on every pretty girl who came into casualty.

Also, I must admit that (partly through my agony uncle columns and partly through my work on the GMC) I've recently come across one or two unpleasant male doctors who've taken advantage of women patients. More of them later in this book – unless, of course, I receive 1,000 quid in used fivers fairly shortly. . . .

I've also known of one or two *women* doctors who've gone to bed with gentlemen patients – they too may feature in the later chapters of this volume, depending on what the publisher's lawyers think. . . .

But for me, it was luckily the case that the issue of nudity was in fact so very trivial that I can remember next to nothing about those adult female patients. I recall far more about my other two charges: a man dying of cancer; and a little girl who kept wriggling.

The man had a vicious form of bone cancer, called multiple myelomatosis. Little treatment was available for it in those days. (It's a bit different now, thank heavens.)

When I first went to see him, he was screaming the place down in agony. He continued to scream day after day almost until the moment he died.

As he was in an uncurtained bed half-way down an open ward, you can imagine the terrible effect of all this on the other patients and their visitors – not to mention on his own family. It was ghastly beyond belief.

What I found particularly hard to accept was the fact that he wasn't given anywhere near enough pain relief to dull his consciousness. With my still very limited medical knowledge, I tried vaguely to query the ethics of allowing a man to undergo such suffering. Couldn't he be given enough morphia or whatever to put him out?

No, I was told – it's not really possible to do that. Crazily enough, the medical and nursing staff seemed to be worried about whether the poor guy was going to get *addicted* to morphia – even though he quite obviously had only a very short time to live. I encountered this attitude again and again over the next few years.

So, instead of giving him sufficient analgesia to keep him in a gentle, drifting state of sleep until death came (a way of treating him which I know would have been *perfectly* possible), we stood around his bed pontificating about his disease.

While he screamed and screamed, our consultant invited me to give a little lecture at his bedside about how I'd detected the particular urinary protein which is characteristic of this disease. It was not a pleasant experience, but at least we were able to walk away from the screaming afterwards – which was more than the nurses or the other patients could do. Thank heavens, he died a few days later.

Nowadays, I'm glad to say, things are managed much better in most places. The great 'hospice movement' has managed to establish the principle that a person who is dying in great pain must be given adequate pain relief. Once the pain has been controlled, the morphia (or whatever) can be reduced a little if necessary. But no one worries too much about whether a man is going to get 'hooked' when it's all too obvious that he'll be dead by Saturday.

On a slightly more cheerful note, the last of my four in-patients was a sweet little girl of about eleven called Carole. One of my main duties with her was to use a syringe and needle to take blood from her arm for tests which I carried out in the ward side-room.

None of us had much idea *how* to take blood at this stage of our student careers – and my difficulties in getting a needle into this child's veins were made far worse by the fact that she couldn't stop wriggling.

That was her problem: *wriggling*.

She'd been doing it for several weeks at home before she came into hospital – and her parents had told her off, ordered her to sit still, and even smacked her a few times.

Then somebody had had the sense to take her to a doctor, who'd correctly diagnosed that she couldn't *help* her wriggling, because it was actually caused by a disease called 'chorea'.

Chorea (pronounced like Korea) is an uncommon childhood variant of rheumatic fever, thought to be due to an odd reaction to a throat germ.

There was really nothing we could do for Carole except keep her in bed and give her some aspirin, while her wriggling gradually got better over four or five weeks. She might as well have been at home, but she was of course a good 'teaching case', so perhaps that was why she was kept in so long.

Unfortunately, during that time I was told to keep on doing what were (quite frankly) rather unnecessary blood tests on her.

So, day after day, I'd go into the ward with a little collecting bottle and a syringe – and stick my needle repeatedly into the poor child's arm.

Why 'repeatedly'? Well you see, like many children (and many plump adults) Carole had no visible veins.

You know how most people's arms have quite prominent blue veins on them. With a few minutes' training, it's quite easy to get into them – which is why most drug addicts can do it without difficulty.

But in a child or in someone ⊢ especially a woman – who's got a slightly plumpish arm, there's often *just nothing to see*.

So what does the doctor do when he wants to take blood?

Fortunately, he knows the approximate location of several arm veins – but it's only 'approximate', because veins are extraordinarily variable in their location. However, there's usually one in front of the elbow joint, and another on the outer side of the forearm.

Furthermore, practice over a period of months or years does enable you to *feel* some invisible veins, using the pad of your finger.

Also, veins can be made more prominent by certain little tricks – like putting a tourniquet round the arm.

But it does take a long time to acquire these skills. And, like the other medical students, I was still a very, very long way off perfecting them. So, morning after morning I went into the ward with my freshly-boiled syringe and needle and attempted to ram the point into one of poor old Carole's totally invisible and impalpable veins.

ME: Don't worry, Carole – I'll try and get it over with quickly.

CAROLE: It hurt a lot yesterday. (*Cries*.)

ME: I'm sorry – I'll try not to hurt today.
(*Jab . . . missed . . . screams*.)

ME: Sorry, love – I'll have to try again.
(*More screams . . . another jab . . . missed again . . . shrieks*.)

Half an hour of this and, as you can imagine, both of us were in a state of abject misery compounded (in her case) with wild hostility and (in mine) with deep guilt.

Carole got better in the end – by herself, and with no medication except aspirin. But when she departed from the ward fully fit (but rather punctured) I was left wondering whether there wasn't some *slightly* better way for medical students to learn how to take blood.

Twenty-five years later, somebody invented a 'multi-vein model arm', made out of plastic and with veins charged with synthetic blood. The idea, of course, is that medics can practise sticking needles in it without hurting anybody.

Alas, it hasn't been widely accepted as yet, so patients continue to be used for target practice by the gallant medical students.

One possible solution to this problem – which makes life in a teaching hospital rather painful for so many patients – would be for medics to practise vein-puncture on each other. The experience of knowing what it's like to be a human pin-cushion would certainly be a salutary one.

Anyway, despite these traumas we ploughed on happily with our six months of swotting on the Medical Firm. Contrary to what many people believe, medical students acquire most of their knowledge *not* through lectures or bedside teaching, but through long hours of 'bashing the textbooks', often far into the night. It's a habit of intense study which (I think understandably) makes doctors contemptuous of the slack learning habits of 'softer' disciplines.

Anyway, by the end of the six months, most of us had read and re-read the 700 pages of Davidson's great *Textbook of Medicine* (plus a lot of lesser volumes as well) and had done our best to commit huge chunks of it to memory. I was very fortunate in the fact that my brain seemed to be able to soak the facts up like a sponge; I take no credit for it, but it certainly made everything from medicine to *Mastermind* a heck of a lot easier.

The bedside teaching on that particular firm was, to be frank, of very variable quality. As is usual in medical schools, there was an obsession with teaching on *rare* cases, and on conditions which most of us would never see again in our lives. The situation is much the same today.

One particular piece of lunacy is that during their time on a Medical Firm, students are often encouraged to concentrate – almost to the exclusion of all else – on *learning to hear heart murmurs*. These are the sounds produced mainly by turbulence in the blood as it rushes through malformed heart valves. In the Victorian and Edwardian days, cardiac specialists who had really sharp ears became almost incredibly skilled at diagnosing abnormalities of the heart valves, simply by listening to these rushing, rumbling and clicking sounds.

We spent endless hours with our stethoscopes stuck on patients' chests, trying desperately to hear those same sounds. We rapidly grasped that to be able to detect them – and then to be able to describe them in loftily impressive terms ('I do believe, sir, that I can hear a mitral diastolic murmur with pre-systolic accentuation, and perhaps an opening snap . . .') – was an excellent way of demonstrating to the consultant that one was a high flyer.

What we did *not* know was that once we went out into

practice, most of us would never really need to detect these esoteric sounds again for the rest of our lives! So we were mostly straining our ears for nothing.

And it *was* a strain, too. Alas, the difficulty of hearing the more obscure heart murmurs was so great that sycophantic or nervous students often lied in their teeth – and *pretended* that they could hear the sounds in order to impress or placate the chief.

In one notable incident, one of our registrars asked a student to listen to a patient's heart, and then demanded to know whether she could hear such-and-such a murmur.

'Oh yes, sir,' replied the hopeful student. 'I can hear it distinctly.'

At this point the registrar gently pointed out to her that the ear-pieces of her stethoscope were actually resting on her *neck*, and not in her ears.

So our fumbling progress on the wards of the Medical Firm was a mixture of comedy and tragedy – just like medicine itself, really. People died, people got better; patients made us laugh and sometimes – with a bit of luck – we made *them* laugh (even when they were dying).

*   *   *

There were two more things that astonished me during those early days of clinical medicine. The first was the fact that so many of the consultants were such extremely poor communicators – both with the patients and with us.

Some of them (including men who subsequently became known as 'among Britain's leading experts on medical education') were almost incoherent as lecturers, with the result that their talks were very poorly attended, and those students who *did* attend often came away muddled and confused. You can imagine how good these chaps must have been at breaking delicate news to patients!

Just in case my recollection is completely wrong about this, I spoke the other day to a doctor friend of mine who'd trained at Glasgow University. His memory of the teaching there is precisely the same: 'the few consultants who were good communicators stand out in the mind, because the rest were so bad at it!'

The other thing that astounded me (and caused me a certain amount of distress) was the discovery that a huge proportion of the patients were, to some degree, emotionally disturbed. In other words, their symptoms were primarily psychological rather than physical.

Our consultants told us this from day one – and initially I refused to believe it. Inwardly, I thought 'Oh, it's just doctors playing the "It's All In Your Mind, Dear" game.'

Unfortunately, from about day six it became increasingly clear that there had to be something in what the consultants said. I remember vividly how an apparently well-adjusted, well-dressed middle-aged man (a bank manager or something similar) came through the consulting-room door with an air of confidence and sat down to talk to me. The moment I asked him 'How are you?' it seemed as though an outer shell of disguise fell from him. Instantly, he launched into a long catalogue of perhaps fifty bizarre symptoms. With the best will in the world, it was difficult to believe that more than half a dozen of them could be physical.

The danger was, of course, that the consultants programmed us (at the very start of our careers) to regard certain symptoms as 'neurotic'. But as the months progressed, I noticed several times that people who'd originally been labelled 'neurotic' ended up dying of cancer. . . .

*　　　*　　　*

One thing that helped to make the death and destruction all the more bearable was the daily contact with the nurses on the ward. For the male medical students (and ninety per cent of us were male), this time which we spent on the Medical Firm was an extraordinary and promise-filled introduction into the crisp, starched, scented world of the nurses.

What an impact they made on us – these elegant,

dedicated and infinitely-desirable young women, trotting efficiently down the wards, black nylons giving audible and erotic evidence of thigh rubbing gently on thigh. . . . No wonder that many a *grande passion*, the odd pregnancy – and even one or two marriages – started on that Medical Firm.

For myself, there were during that time one or two *passions* – enjoyable and infinitely soothing, if not actually *grandes*.

I make no apology for saying that one of the reasons that I coped reasonably well with those months of dealing with life and death was that solace could be found in the arms of the nurses – and sometimes in the (slightly more muscular) arms of the physiotherapists.

Alas, my long relationship with my dear, sweet girl-friend – who I had loved so much, and who had helped me with her love through the difficult years of dissection and animal experiment – was coming to an end.

She had left school and enrolled as a student nurse at another teaching hospital a long distance away. The life was tough there, and the sisters in charge of the nurses' home treated their girls a bit like convicts on a one-way ticket to Botany Bay. They were, perhaps understandably, desperately keen to protect the young ladies' sexual morals. One Home Sister in particular took this responsibility so seriously that she used to go through the nurses' lockers and inspect their knickers! (I'm not quite sure what for.)

This really was about the last straw for my girl-friend – a bright butterfly of a lass who'd already found the stresses of dealing with blood, pus, excrement, vomit and death a little difficult, to say the least.

Very wisely, she eventually retired from the nursing profession and went off to be a television presenter – a job in which, I am glad to say, the bosses do not go round inspecting your knickers.

At least, not at the BBC.

7

SURGERY AND SEX

AND NOW, on to the Surgical Firm. My first morning in the operating theatre was absolutely wonderful.

If I tell you that I am a total big-head (Goodness! Had you guessed already?), you will not be surprised to learn that what I immediately remember about the occasion was the sight of myself, reflected in a glass partition – standing in front of the operating table and wearing (drama! drama!) a surgeon's cap, gown and mask. I was *most* impressed.

In fact, I didn't take any part in the operation – which was just as well, since I was obviously lost in admiration of the image of myself looking a bit like that nice Dr Kildare on the telly.

To be more serious, I found the sight of the operation quite magnificent. It was for the removal of a thyroid: that's the big, butterfly-shaped gland which lies in the front of your neck, just below your Adam's apple.

The patient, Mrs Hay, was one of the little batch who were under my tender if inept care on the wards. She'd suffered from an over-active thyroid for some years and, like countless other women with this common condition, she'd become thin, bird-like and nervy, with protruding eyes and shaking hands.

There are three ways of treating an over-active thyroid: tablets; radiotherapy; and surgery. Tablets hadn't worked for her, and radiotherapy had been ruled out because she was still of child-bearing age, and the radiation might have damaged her ovaries.

So, the answer was to remove her thyroid surgically. Though this is a very common operation, it's actually a very tricky and delicate one. Why? Because if the surgeon makes any mistakes in where he's cutting, he can easily leave the patient with problems like having no voice for the rest of her life.

And, I assure you, such mistakes do happen. Every thyroid surgeon dreads the day when he cuts through the nerve that supplies the patient's voice-box.

Anyway, this particular surgeon was a great man. He was actually a *rectal* surgeon, and because he had certain royal connections plus a knighthood, he was known to us students as The Hereditary Keeper of the Back Passage.

It may surprise you that a rectal surgeon was taking out somebody's thyroid (the neck, as you may have noticed, being rather a long way from the bottom). But this bloke (who I'll call Sir Murrayfield) was so dextrous that I daresay he could have operated on any bit of the body, and done it beautifully.

I watched in admiration as Sir Murrayfield slowly and calmly began by painting the unconscious patient's neck with golden iodine. Then, without any fuss or drama, he neatly clipped a series of sterile green towels over the painted skin, so that just a small rectangle of Mrs Hay was left exposed.

I remember vividly the startling contrast between the gold of her iodine-painted neck and the reassuring green of the surrounding towels. Then the surgeon added another colour: blood red.

A horizontal scarlet line appeared across the front of the throat as he made the first incision. To my relief I didn't faint (a common reaction among medical students), and I didn't feel at all sick either.

Instead, I was just totally fascinated as I watched Sir

Murrayfield and his assistant deftly stop the blood flow by applying small pairs of forceps to the bleeding points, and then tying neat little knots of catgut round them. In a matter of a minute or two, the blood loss was virtually at an end. Sir Murrayfield pressed on, dissecting his way through the yellow fat and down to the plump, purple thyroid itself.

After half an hour of slow, meticulous work, he'd gently freed the thyroid from the adjoining structures – taking time to point out to me the crucial nerve to the voice-box, which might so easily have been cut by someone in a rush. Then, without hurry, he set about removing nine-tenths of the thyroid. (It's important to *leave* a tenth, because otherwise the patient would thenceforward produce no thyroid hormone at all, and would spend the rest of her life in a state of thyroid deficiency.) He also took care not to damage the *para*thyroid glands – four or five tiny structures located in the back of the thyroid itself.

Finally, the meticulous dissection process was over, and Sir Murrayfield lifted the unwanted thyroid out of Mrs Hay's neck and dropped it casually, like a small dark glove, into a metal dish.

Then slowly, gently, almost lovingly, he began to 'close up' the layers of tissue – finishing by bringing the two cut edges of skin together and deftly fastening them across the front of Mrs H's throat with a neat row of tiny metal clips, rather than stitches.

It had been a masterly performance. And when, a week or so later, I helped remove Mrs Hay's skin clips, it was apparent that as a result of the delicacy with which he'd placed them, she would have virtually no visible scar across the front of her neck. I need hardly add that she was *cured* – and that she didn't lose her voice!

Oddly enough, Sir Murrayfield's technique was in stark contrast to that of another surgeon who I watched take out a thyroid some months later at another hospital. This man was supposed to be one of the world's leading thyroid surgeons; yet compared with Sir Murrayfield, he seemed like a navvy with three thumbs. Perhaps I just caught him on an off day, but the experience did teach me that surgeons do vary quite remarkably in their techniques and skills, and that it pays to find a good one.

My second experience in the operating theatre was somewhat less aesthetic and decidedly more robust. Skip this para if you've got a weak stomach, but it involved the amputation of the lower half of a leg. It was done with flourish and panache by a jolly sort of orthopaedic surgeon who looked rather like Fred Astaire. With a few swift sweeps of the knife and a quick hack with the saw just below the knee, he had the whole thing off in no time – leaving me to carry it away (like a heavy wellington boot) and dump it somewhere on the far side of the theatre.

Again, I experienced no faintness or revulsion (unlike one or two of my colleagues, who felt quite ill), and I was profoundly grateful for that. After the years in which I'd reacted so badly to dissection of corpses, it seemed that I was now developing a stronger stomach. But there were other hurdles to be faced in the near future. . . .

* * *

So there I was in my third year of medical studies, now aged twenty-one, and just starting out on a six months' spell on the Surgical Firm.

The firm was led by a large and formidable consultant surgeon whose name was something like Mr Waldegrave-Bendall. Many of our surgeons had impressive double-barrelled handles like that; hardly any of them ever had simple names like 'John Bloggs' – because of the fact that, fairly early on, they'd mostly realised that sticking an unusual extra moniker in before the surname was a useful way of advancing one's surgical career. For the same reason, at least two of my classmates got themselves hyphenated when they qualified, so as to avoid the anonymity of being a mere 'Dr Smith'.

W.-B. was a powerful silver-haired man, who wore the

half-moon glasses favoured by so many elderly surgeons. He was remarkably dextrous, despite having no index finger on his right hand.

You may wonder how anyone with a (fairly essential) finger missing could be a top surgeon. But he'd learned to cope, thanks to the nimbleness of his other fingers. In fact there were a number of fine operators of W.-B.'s generation who, like him, had missing digits: the reason being that they had started surgical practice in an era when antibiotics hadn't been invented. Therefore, if you cut yourself while operating, you could be in real trouble – for if germs from the patient got in, you stood an appreciable chance of losing a finger or (if you were unlucky) of dying from blood poisoning. W.-B. had survived the septic finger of his early surgical years, and had become one of the best and most respected operators of his day.

For me, to help him at an operation was a pleasure and a privilege – even though he was an irascible old devil. I should explain that surgeons *need* help at almost all operations, because one pair of hands isn't really enough – especially if you've got a few digits missing already. Indeed, with *larger* operations, it's better to have three or four pairs of hands inside your patient.

You see, while the surgeon actually does the delicate dissecting and cutting, his assistants help by doing such things as putting clamps on spurting blood vessels, mopping up blood with swabs, touching bleeding points with the diathermy (a hot probe that seals up blood vessels by sizzling them), hauling on retractors (things a bit like bent fish-slices which you use to pull bits of bowel and other organs back out of the way), trimming catgut sutures inside the hole, and – if you were *very* lucky! – doing a bit of stitching too.

I loved it.

Fully scrubbed-up and dressed in sterile gown and gloves, I spent many happy hours giving my somewhat clumsy help to Mr W.-B. and, more importantly, watching as his delicate nine-fingered pair of hands cut and probed their way down into abdomen after abdomen.

*   *   *

The programme for a morning's operating was very much the same then as it is now. We'd come into the surgeons' changing room, take off everything except our underwear, put on freshly-laundered green theatre pyjamas and short white wellington boots, and then don masks and of course surgical caps – in an attempt to keep any stray germs in our hair from falling into the patient. (My major problem was stopping my *glasses* from falling into the patient.)

Those who were actually taking part in the operation, as opposed to just watching, would then 'scrub up' – an agreeable process, reminiscent of scenes in a hundred B-movies (and even some A-movies), in which we spent a relaxing five minutes in a little wash-room scrubbing intensively from the finger-nails to the elbows, finally finishing with that authoritative surgeon's gesture of switching off the taps with the inside of your arms (it avoids contaminating your hands with germs from the tap handle).

If I was 'scrubbing up', then my next move would be to pick up a green sterile gown and thrust my newly-scrubbed arms into it. Immediately (a real ego-booster this!), a solicitous nurse would materialise behind me and tie the gown for me at the back; the *front* of the gown always has to remain sterile, you see, while the back doesn't.

Finally, I'd slip my hands into a pair of sterile rubber gloves – using a neat little surgeon's trick to make sure that I didn't touch the outsides – and then draw them up over my sterile sleeves. On a good day, I'd achieve this without actually bursting the glove.

Now, hands held high to avoid contamination, I'd advance to the table alongside the surgeon – and battle would commence.

Actually, 'battle' certainly wasn't the right word for it (unless Waldegrave-Bendall chose to have a tiff with the theatre sister or some unfortunate member of her staff and throw a knife on the floor in a fit of pique). For, contrary to what you might think from watching films or TV medicated soap-operas, the atmosphere in the average theatre is, of necessity, *not* drama-charged, but calm and almost casual.

The patient is normally wheeled in already unconscious, followed very closely by the anaesthetist with his little trolley of gas cylinders and monitoring gear. There's a slight flurry as the porters strain to lift him on to the table (the patient, that is, not the anaesthetist), and then everything settles down.

In no time, the skin is painted, the green drapes are on, and the anaesthetist tells the surgeon that it's OK to go ahead. If he's wrong, the first cut will be rapidly followed by a sharp raising of the unconscious patient's knees as he attempts to walk straight back to the ward. The involuntary spasm usually tips all the instruments on to the floor, so that they have to be taken away to be re-sterilized. Understandably, surgeons are not best pleased when this happens.

After the preliminaries, all is amiably chatty and tranquil. The operation progresses peacefully, with the surgeon snipping away, sometimes directing his juniors' attention to a point of interest, but more often discussing last night's TV or airing his views on politics. These politics may well be very much to the right of centre – but it'd be a bold junior who would disagree with his chief's opinion on the government or the trade unions.

So, things proceed. There is the clang of instrument on kidney dish, the frying noise of the diathermy, and the constant reassuring sound of the patient's breath echoing through the anaesthetist's tubes.

In fact, in most of the bigger operations the anaesthetist takes over the patient's breathing for him completely – either pumping the gas in and out of him in the old, traditional way with a hand-held rubber bag, or else doing the same thing with an automatic pumping machine. Why? Because life is much easier for the surgeon if the patient has been temporarily *paralysed* by a drug injected by the anaesthetist. This makes his body totally relaxed, so that the surgeon can poke about inside him without encountering spasms of muscular resistance.

It is unfortunately true that very rarely (but *less* rarely in Caesarean operations, for which the anaesthetic is very light), the poor old patient is paralysed as I've described, but remains just about conscious, though unable to indicate to anyone that he or she is awake and feeling pain. This really should not happen unless the anaesthetist is pretty half-asleep himself.

Anyway, don't let the above alarm you. Although headline-hitting anaesthetic disasters ('Boy turned into vegetable through carelessness') do, alas, occur – particularly in badly-staffed and badly-equipped hospitals – all the teaching hospital anaesthetists I've ever met are immensely sensible, reliable men and women, not given to nodding off or indulging in sudden whims or tantrums (you can see how their personalities differ from those of their surgical colleagues!). Quietly efficient and never ruffled, they sit there, pumping away, injecting the odd carefully thought-out potion, calming the surgeon down if he gets irritable and – in those days – doing *The Times* or *Telegraph* crossword with the other hand.

A remarkable breed of sanguine men and women, into whose hands (I reckon) you can safely entrust your life. . . .

*   *   *

Back to the surgeon: what sort of cases is he actually *doing* during the morning's session?

Well, Mr Waldegrave-Bendall's morning 'menu' was pretty typical of what most general surgeons would tackle in the course of a strenuous four, five or six hour session before a brief lunch. It was drawn up a couple of days previously by his young house surgeon, and it usually looked something like this:

MR WALDEGRAVE-BENDALL'S OPERATING LIST

1. **Private In-growing Toenail**   This would be the only non-NHS case of the morning, and W.-B. would be picking up a hundred quid or so for it. Traditionally, private patients went *first* on the list. Equally traditionally, us fawning medical students grovelled in their eagerness to assist the surgeon with such cases – in the rather vain hope that he'd *remember*, and offer us jobs one day.

2. **Gall Bladder Removal**   This was W.-B.'s *pièce-de-résistance* – a major operation at which he was absolutely brilliant. He could remove a gall bladder with great delicacy and skill in one hour flat – meanwhile commenting on how the bungling of Sir Anthony Eden's 'gall bag' removal by a less-gifted surgeon had:

(i)   ruined the British Prime Minister's health;
(ii) led to the appalling misjudgement of the Suez fiasco; and
(iii) done irreparable harm to the Anglo-American alliance.

I am inclined to say he was right on all counts: if W.-B. had been the man who took out Eden's gall bladder, the whole history of the relationship between Britain and America (and, of course, the troubled relationship between Britain and the Arab world) would have been far, far different. Honest.

3. **Gastrectomy**   This means removal of the stomach (for ulcers or cancer): a difficult and physically demanding operation, not so much

performed now that we have much better anti-
ulcer drugs. I remember it as being bloody and
exhausting for everybody (including the patient).

4. **Hemicolectomy** Removal of half the large
bowel, usually for cancer. A massive, tiring
operation, often involving the 'fashioning' of a
colostomy opening in the skin of the abdomen.

5. **Excision of Breast Lump** With a bit of luck,
this might *not* 'proceed' to a mastectomy – if the
pathologist's urgent telephone report from the lab
said the lump was benign.

6. **Hernia** Rupture – an undemanding operation, which the great man might begin, and then
leave to his house surgeon or registrar to finish off
while he himself went in search of a well-earned
sandwich.

Not a bad morning's work for an elderly gent, eh?

*   *   *

You can see from all this that just about the most important
quality needed to be a surgeon was (and to my mind still is)
sheer physical *endurance*.

To stand up for hours in a humid operating theatre, often
sweating profusely, wading your way through blood,
tugging on instruments, attempting to spot delicate structures with your long-sighted middle-aged eyes, taking
decisions which could mean life or death to certain
patients, trying to control a surgical team of varying
degrees of eptitude, and doing a bit of teaching on the side
. . . all of this was (and is) enormously draining.

Even today, I know many surgeons who put in a
punishingly long morning session like the one I've
described – and who then snatch a ham roll and a cup of
coffee before knocking off a couple of appendixes and a

case of piles. After that, they nip down to their out-patients
clinic, whip through about twenty-five people, grab a cup of
tea, do a ward round, look in on a committee meeting
which might affect their personal 'empires', dictate a dozen
letters, go home for a brief bite of supper – then head off to
the local *private* nursing home at about 8 p.m. to rip
through (if you'll forgive the phrase) a fairly lucrative
evening operating list until midnight. And so to bed.

Indeed, before leaving the house at 6.30 a.m. to fit in
another couple of private cases, some of them probably
remember to make love to their wives. Possibly twice.

You can now perhaps see why surgeons are almost
invariably Type A personalities.

*   *   *

I wrote part of this chapter while on an extremely wearing
trip across the Andes with a party of about twenty
surgeons. Virtually all of them (male and female) were
opinionated, loud, arrogant, wildly insensitive to the
feelings of the peasants around them – but also extremely
funny and *totally* indomitable! They battled bravely from
Brazil through Bolivia to Peru, coping with diarrhoea and
with altitude sickness (for which they had brought no
remedies because, being surgeons, they'd never heard of
it). As far as I can recall, none of them ever offered any
word of complaint whatever. I have to admire the Surgical
Personality.

*   *   *

Anyway, surgery wasn't *all* blood and thunder and physical
exhaustion. Part of the fascination of it was the sheer
detective work involved. Let me explain.

A man would come into our hospital, bright yellow with
unexplained jaundice. There are at least fifty reasons why a
chap might go yellow, and the object of admitting him was
to find out just which one applied to him.

So I'd examine him; and the young house surgeon would

examine him; and perhaps the senior registrar would examine him too. Maybe all this would give us some clue as to the cause of his jaundice – gall-stones perhaps, or hepatitis, or cirrhosis of the liver, or cancer?

Next the house surgeon would tell me to do some tests on the man's blood and his urine, and maybe check the colour of his faeces (we were always knee-deep in faeces of varying hues and aromas).

From the results, we'd be a step nearer to sorting out the puzzle. Usually, something was blocking the flow of his bile, damming it back so that it entered his blood, so staining his skin and his eyes yellow. We all put forward our explanations – rather as if we were in the penultimate scene of an Agatha Christie mystery.

But the great thing was that we knew that, sure as fate, the denouement would take place next Tuesday morning in the operating theatre. On that day, like the Detective Inspector Who Reveals All (or the question master who takes the correct answer out of the sealed envelope), Mr W.-B. would pick up his knife, slit open the top right-hand corner of the patient's abdomen – and there was the answer.

With good luck, it would be a pearly gall-stone, jamming the chap's bile duct. With *less* good luck, I'm afraid, it would be a vile-looking cancer of the pancreas, which there was little hope of curing – only of palliating.

You may think it awful that, in some ways, we regarded all this as a fascinating puzzle – a game in which the winner was the one whose diagnosis was correct when the man's abdomen was opened.

But surgery was ever thus and I'm afraid it always will be. We'd already learned that life was harsh, and that a proportion of our patients were doomed to die. We'd also learned that the best way to cope with it was to regard much of it as a challenge to the intellect – or (at other times) as a bit of a joke.

A joke? When someone is dying of cancer?

Yes, I'm afraid so. Medicine and (to a much lesser extent) nursing are the only professions in which cancer is discreetly regarded as a subject suitable for joking – in order, of course, to make the job bearable.

I'm sorry if that upsets a lot of the people who read this book – after all, since *one in five* of us dies of cancer, almost everyone has lost a relative to carcinoma. But there we are: if you live with it, and work with it and see its ghastly effects every day, what else can you do but joke about it? During the time I was finishing this chapter (late 1988), I took part in a debate at a learned medical society – at which a speaker from the floor brought the house down with a joke about cancer.

Ghastly? Ghoulish? No, not really. It was a simple story about a very slow surgeon. At the end of a long operation, the anaesthetist asked him if he'd checked for secondary cancer deposits in the liver.

'I did at the beginning,' said the surgeon ponderously.

'I know,' said the anaesthetist, 'but I just thought that there might be some *by now*. . . .'

To any reader whose wife or husband has just died of cancer, such a jest must seem quite unforgivable. Yet to most of today's doctors, such jokes make the whole horrific thing bearable. And, equally, that was the case with us medical students, back in 1960 or '61, struggling to cope with the ghastly facts of life and death.

*   *   *

Similarly, to you reading this book, it must seem unbelievable that while a patient was being opened up in the theatre, the student who was helping at the operation might perhaps be thinking more about the beautiful eyes of the masked nurse standing opposite him than about whether the man on the table was going to recover. But that's how it was. The girls in their masks and thin theatre gowns occupied our minds very much – especially on hot summer days when they wore only the skimpiest of underwear, so that their soft, musky, feminine aromas all too readily took one's mind off the finer points of repairing a rupture.

Indeed the appearance and tantalizing scent of these harem-like beauties was so exotic that countless dates were discreetly arranged in the corners of the operating theatre. It's regrettably true that some of the girls with whom we made these romantic assignations turned out to be slightly *less* lovely when they removed their masks – but never mind.

Sadly, because most medical students knew absolutely nothing about sex or contraception (they were only training to be *doctors*, after all), a lot of those liaisons ran into disaster. Nurses seemed to be perpetually deciding they were pregnant – and quite often they were right. This crazy situation was uniform throughout the teaching hospitals: at Bart's, it was claimed that if you took a sample of the water in the nurses' swimming-pool, it would give a positive pregnancy test.

The results of all that ignorant and unprotected groping were sad: some nurses went off and had ghastly 'back street' abortions; others were discreetly taken care of by consultant gynaecologists who were willing to do a rather more extensive 'appendicectomy' than usual.

And, inevitably, quite a number of nurses very hastily married students or young doctors 'because they had to'. How foolish that many a medical marriage got started in this way – especially as we now know that such shotgun marriages are appreciably more likely to end in divorce.

Looking back, I'm a little surprised that the girls were so willing to give their lovely bodies to the boys – because the love-making techniques of the average beer-swilling, rugby-playing medical student appeared to be pretty rudimentary.

Many of the lads *still* didn't seem to know where the clitoris was, because we hadn't done 'gynae' yet (that's in the next chapter but one). And some of them seemed to think that any attempt at foreplay was decidedly unmanly:

what a chap was supposed to do was to ram it in as hard as possible; what a girl was supposed to do was *be grateful*. Ye gods!

*   *   *

Our general fog of ignorance didn't make it any easier for us medics to cope with the sexual and emotional queries which the patients were now presenting to us on the wards. I regret to say that the standard response at that period to that kind of query was just to brush it aside.

But sometimes the patients' sexual responses couldn't be *totally* ignored – as my friend Jake found out to his chagrin. Part of our job was to shave all patients pre-operatively, from the nipples to the knees. (This dotty and uncomfortable ritual was enforced with great rigor, because it was believed that it was vital in order to prevent infection: it has now been largely abandoned.)

Jake went to the wards one night to shave off a middle-aged man's body hair with a cut-throat razor. But while depriving the unfortunate bloke of his 'pubes', he found to his embarrassment that the stimulation was giving the patient an unwanted erection.

Very unwisely, my friend continued with the shave – with the result that the patient ended up by 'coming' over Jake's razor hand!

The patient seemed to be as mortified as the medical student was by this sudden deluge. As Jake tried to mop himself up, he heard the poor man saying, 'I expect you doctors have this sort of thing happening to you *all* the time.'

We fervently hoped not. . . .

8

CASUALTY!

'LISTEN — CASUALTY'S NO place for the squeamish! You get people carted in there bleedin' to death, with their legs driven up through their shoulders.'

The speaker was a medical student six months ahead of me. As I wasn't sure how I was going to be able to cope with the blood and thunder of working in the busy Casualty department, I'd approached him for a little preliminary reassurance. (Gulp!)

Every student doctor has to spend several weeks working in a Casualty department, day and night, learning how to deal with the injured, the assaulted, the poisoned, the hypochondriacal, and the downright insane. That was what I had to do next.

I knew that into our Casualty department flowed each day a steady stream of victims of appalling road accidents, some of whom were at death's door – and some of whom were unfortunately well through it. Was I going to be able to cope?

Well, as with everything else which we'd faced until then, it turned out that Casualty was 'copable with'. You needed a strong stomach to be untroubled by the vomit, excrement, violence and blood of an action-packed Saturday night. But late on one of those first hectic nights came a moment when I realised I had nothing to fear now.

A middle-aged man had been brought in, horribly mangled by a road accident. You'll probably be surprised to hear that I can't recall the precise details – but the volume of patients who we saw in Casualty was so vast (literally hundreds a day) that they defy memory.

Anyway, I've a vague recollection that the unfortunate guy was unconscious, had badly smashed legs and was bleeding heavily, and that the qualified doctors were desperately trying to put up drips and stop the torrential blood flow.

Meanwhile, I (the gallant student) was up at the head end, attempting to maintain an 'airway' so that the poor bloke could breathe.

In the midst of all this, he was violently sick – *straight into my eyes*.

A moment later, I was delighted to note that I had reacted merely by giving a quick chuckle at my own expense – after which I rapidly wiped my eyes, and got on with helping to save his life.

So you can see that by this stage, all us medics had learned to be pretty tough! Like the nurses, we'd become inured to the unpleasantness of certain of the body's less agreeable products. For the rest of our lives, we would be relatively undisturbed by the sight of a fellow human throwing up, passing water, struck down by diarrhoea – or having a colossal haemorrhage. (Admittedly, I'm not too keen on people doing some of these things while I'm having my dinner, but there we are.)

Indeed, a couple of years later – by which time I was qualified – I remember trying unsuccessfully to save a man who'd just dropped dead in the ward with a heart attack. I got a plastic airway into his mouth and was blowing into it – in other words, giving him the 'kiss of life' – when another young doctor started enthusiastic and forceful cardiac massage. The effect of his first violent thrust on the lower end of the breastbone was to send the contents of the poor old patient's stomach straight into my mouth.

Appalling as it may seem to you, once again our only reaction was to laugh (obviously I spat the muck out into a basin first). We carried on trying to save the chap, but failed. After that I went and washed my mouth out and, as far as I remember, we pushed off to lunch.

No doctor would find anything in the least surprising in the fact that I hadn't really lost my appetite.

*   *   *

The job of a student in Casualty was very exciting. The place was run by a group of young doctors who were mostly hoping to make a career as surgeons. Surprisingly, in view of the vast number of serious injuries which poured in each day, there were never any consultants in Casualty to supervise things. If your life was going to be saved, it would be saved by a young registrar or a houseman – or possibly a student. Indeed, in the dark reaches of the night the whole of Casualty might be in the care of only one twenty-three-year-old house surgeon.

Under these circumstances, resident medical students were gladly welcomed by the hard-pressed docs – who gratefully delegated large amounts of work to us.

Stitching wounds, for instance: on day one I spent half an hour or so watching the young Casualty officer suture some gashes, and was then left to get on with it myself for the first time.

Well, I enjoyed it *enormously*. I have a vague recollection of my very first stitching case: a young man with his scalp split wide open by a bottle or some other blunt instrument. I put him on the operating table in the little Casualty theatre, then donned a plastic apron and 'scrubbed up' (feeling splendidly important!).

Assisted by a nurse, I cleaned carefully all round the patient's cut, and trimmed back his hair an inch or so from the sides of it.

Next, I drew up a syringeful of local anaesthetic and cautiously injected it all round the chap's scalp wound – in order to deaden it. I was agreeably surprised to find that giving him the jab of 'local' only made him grunt *slightly* with pain. (Later, I found that there was virtually no discomfort at all if you shoved the injection needle in *through* the gaping wound, instead of through the skin itself.)

Now: a pause of a couple of minutes to let the local anaesthetic take effect. Meanwhile, nurse and I were doing our best to calm down the patient, who was getting into a state of alcoholic agitation (half the people in Casualty seemed to be drunk – at least in the evenings).

Come to think of it, the guy would have been even more agitated if he'd known that this was the first wound I'd treated. Anyway, eventually came the moment when I picked up my needle and thread in a sort of 'gripping' instrument (like a pair of pliers, really) and nonchalantly drove the tip into his skin.

To my relief, he *didn't* jump off the couch, but just continued boozily chatting as I shoved the stitching needle through the surprisingly tough flesh on one side of his cut. Next, with an effort, I forced the point up through the skin on the other side, tied a neat knot – and I was in business! Ten minutes later, I'd stitched the entire wound together.

I cannot tell you how satisfying this sort of thing was to all of us students. In my case, it wasn't just that I fancied myself at embroidery (I was slightly unusual among boys in that my Mum had given me a sewing machine when I was four). No, it was more a question of the sheer satisfaction of *putting something right for somebody quickly and neatly*.

I really think that that's one of the major reasons why people become doctors and (in most cases) enjoy remaining as doctors: there's a remarkable sense of fulfilment in 'sorting out' something for someone who's in trouble, by using whatever expertise you've got.

That principle applied to my first tentative attempts at stitching up bottle wounds (attempts which improved when I realised there was a better, neater way of sewing, which brought the skin-edges together so that the joins would scarcely show). I think it also applied to the efforts of the hard-pressed Casualty doctors and nurses, who took considerable pride in the efficiency with which they pumped out the stomachs of the endless stream of poor devils who'd tried to kill themselves with an overdose of barbiturates.

It applied also to the surgeons to whom we handed over so many of our Casualty cases, once we'd carried out the immediate (and often life-saving) manoeuvres: they seemed to me to be justifiably proud of the efficiency with which they re-aligned shattered bones, or swiftly opened a skull to remove a deadly blood clot.

The feeling that you can do something to *help* somebody is a heady and agreeable one – which, I am convinced, permeates the medical and nursing professions. If you have a nurse as a girl-friend, you'll find that (unlike other women) she'll be absolutely *delighted* if you have a boil or a spot on your back – because what she will want to do most in all the world is to squeeze or lance it for you!

And if you marry (say) a plastic surgeon, and are unwise enough to complain about any bits of your body, you'll probably find that for the rest of your lives, he'll scarcely be able to restrain himself from enlarging your boobs, 'lifting' your face, or aspirating fat from your thighs. These things will give him great satisfaction.

You may well disagree with my personal theory of what motivates most doctors (and nurses). 'What about *dedication*?' I hear you ask.

Well, neither in Casualty nor anywhere else did I hear any of my fellow-students actually mention 'dedication' as a reason for what they were doing with such pleasure. I felt that there were one or two gentle, religious boys and girls who genuinely *were* dedicated to improving the lot of suffering humanity – though without making a big fuss about it. They tended, not surprisingly, to go on to do missionary work after they qualified.

But I have to add that in a lifetime of practice – including ten years sitting on the medical profession's disciplinary body, the GMC – the only doctors I've encountered who told people that they were *dedicated* had just one thing in common.

They were all scoundrels.

*   *   *

On about day four of my first week in Casualty, we were told that an emergency ambulance was coming into the courtyard with an unconscious woman aboard.

The senior Casualty doctor (a chap of about twenty-five) and I hopped swiftly outside and entered the vehicle. Within it lay a plump, cheerful-looking middle-aged house-wife. Her bright pink complexion contrasted sharply with her rather awful electric-blue nightie. She looked a nice sort of soul, I thought.

I certainly wasn't worried about her. We'd had a couple of dozen unconscious people come in by ambulance during my first few days on Casualty – and in every case the 'Cas. officers' had worked out a diagnosis (for instance, head injury, drug overdose, diabetes, alcohol intoxication or hysteria) and had given the appropriate treatment. I was getting used to seeing people 'come round', and say the right things like 'Where am I?' and 'Gorblessyou, doc' – and I confidently expected that that was what would happen here.

The senior Cas. officer simply inspected the back of the lady's eyes with an instrument, then handed it to me.

'You might like to have a look,' he said. 'That appearance of spasm in the blood vessels is very common.'

Then he turned and started to wander out of the ambulance. Over his shoulder he added, 'She's dead, of course.'

I was thunderstruck. The woman looked so pink and well. (Later, I realised that her pinkness was caused by the gas from the cooker that she'd put her head in – a common method of suicide in those days.) Yet she was gone. There was nothing to be done but look in her eyes for the signs of death, and then let the ambulance driver take her round to the mortuary.

It was a shock to find that here was something we could not 'put right' in Casualty: namely, being dead.

*　　　*　　　*

As I said earlier, intervening in order to put patients' problems right is a heady business, and it's easy to get carried away with it.

Though our Casualty department was basically intended to be a place where patients came in situations of real emergency, somehow or other we'd got also into the habit of operating on people's painful in-growing toenails. Students were let loose to carry out this barbaric procedure on about their fifth day in Casualty.

I use the word 'barbaric' because it's now widely recognised that the crude operation which we were carrying out at that time was totally useless. It involved deadening the big toe with a couple of jabs of 'local' neatly placed into the nerves at the base of the toe – after which, we simply ripped half the toenail off!

Awfully satisfying to a medical student, of course (even if a trifle alarming to the patient). But it did absolutely no good – because the toenail soon re-grew and usually started causing the same pains as before. (I only found this out when I was mad enough to let another student operate on *my* in-growing toenail.)

Still, the technique which we'd learned in deadening the nerves to the big toe was a useful one, and in next to no time we were using it to deaden people's *fingers* as well – so that we could stitch up gashes in their fingertips or open up pus-filled swellings around their fingernails.

From time immemorial, young (and old) surgeons have derived great satisfaction from plunging a knife into a great, painful collection of pus and letting it all out. Alas, one of my student friends came badly unstuck in his very first week on Casualty while trying to do just that to a patient with an abscess on his fingertip. The results were tragic.

What happened? The bottles which contained the local anaesthetic were stored all mixed up with absolutely identical-looking bottles which contained exactly the same stuff – *plus adrenaline*. (Confusion between bottles is a recurring theme in medical accidents, I'm afraid.)

Adrenaline makes blood vessels close down, so the mixture of 'local' plus adrenaline was often used on heavily bleeding scalp wounds, in order to reduce the flow.

Unfortunately, my friend John stuck *this* mixture into the base of his patient's finger, in mistake for pure local anaesthetic. It certainly numbed the finger all right, but it did a little more than that. Thanks to the effect of the adrenaline, the finger went gangrenous – and eventually dropped off.

Not too good for the patient, eh? And not too good for poor old student John – who felt that the GMC were probably going to strike him off before he'd even been struck on.

Did the patient sue the hospital? God knows, but I don't think so. Among the welter of human disasters that passed before our eyes each day and night, this was only one tiny item. As a student, I had no time to enquire about the final outcome of the case: it was on with the next ten stitchings, the next five coronaries and the next three overdoses.

Unbelievable as it may seem to you, although I even saw a *murdered* man one night, I had no chance of following the case up or of finding out whether the police had got anybody for the crime. All I remember is a big chap being rushed in, and a Casualty officer saying, 'It's no good – he's already dead.'

I stood behind the patient's head, looking down at him. He seemed perfectly healthy, except that he was extremely still – and also there was a tiny, tiny hole in the left side of his chest. It was so small that I could scarcely have put a ball-point pen into it, but the wounded Mercutio's dying words in *Romeo and Juliet* ran through my mind:

> No, 'tis not so deep as a well, nor so wide as a church door – but 'tis enough, 'twill serve.

All we could discover before we shipped the poor dead young man off to the freezer room was that someone had jabbed him just once in the chest – with a screwdriver. A seemingly innocuous blow but, unfortunately, the tip had gone straight into his heart. I made a mental resolve *never* to fight anyone who was carrying a sharp instrument.

* * *

In sharp contrast, a heck of a lot of what came through Casualty was what we loftily called 'clag' – in other words, trivia.

People would wander in claiming to have been bitten by spiders (there are, of course, *no* biting spiders in Britain); others would pop in because 'all of a sudden I coughed, doctor'; still others felt that the Casualty department was the place to take their pimples or their athlete's foot. One woman queued for perhaps an hour: when she finally got to the head of the queue, she demanded a pair of our surgical gloves to do her washing up with! (And became *very* hostile when I refused.)

Equally crazily, people staggered into Casualty at two in the morning, indignantly demanding investigations for indigestion which they'd had for months or even years.

D'you think I'm being harsh? Well, doubtless these people all thought that the accident and emergency department of a teaching hospital was the correct place to get their long-term medical problems sorted out. Contrariwise, the infuriated Casualty officers (and us, their intrepid medical students) firmly believed that Casualty was a place to which one brought Dramatic Accidents (and the bigger the better), rather than spots on one's bottom.

To be honest, the situation in Casualty (with the doctors

being furious with half the punters for coming along at all!) was made worse by the truly appalling standard of some of the GPs who practised near the hospital.

While there are, of course, some really superb general practitioners around, the fact is that some of the weaker brethren who had surgeries near to our Casualty were unbelievably bad. Among their favourite habits were:

closing the surgery for the day, and leaving a note on the door saying 'If you are ill, go to the hospital Casualty department';

sending patients up to Casualty with an NHS prescription form (!) on which were written only the laconic words 'Please see and treat';

simply refusing to answer their phones, so that anybody who was sick had little alternative but to make his or her way up to Casualty.

Things have improved enormously in British general practice over the last twenty-five years or so, and a doctor who tried to pull those kind of stunts today would probably find himself being 'done' by me and my colleagues on the GMC.

But I still treasure the memory of one of our legendary local GPs of the 1960s, Dr Merdecul – who, according to Casualty department folklore, had given his name to a new 'clinical sign.'

What the 'clinical sign' consisted of was this. Dr Merdecul was one of the last practitioners in Britain to have a speaking tube in his porch. If you rang his doorbell in the middle of the night and gasped into the speaking tube that you had a pain in your tummy, then (so it was alleged) Dr Merdecul would reply, 'Please put your right hand in your trouser pocket.'

And if you did this and then said '*Ow!*' – well, Dr Merdecul would immediately announce, 'You have acute appendicitis. I will throw you a referral letter out of the window and you will please take it immediately to Casualty.'

Unfortunately, this story was only a mild exaggeration of the truth. Very large numbers of patients were sent in to the department by GPs (admittedly hard-pressed GPs) who had never examined them and, in some cases, never even *seen* them. Understandably, a certain bitterness developed between the Casualty officers and the minority of really bad local general practitioners. (In contrast, everyone welcomed a referral from one of the *good* local family doctors with open arms.)

* * *

An additional and massive problem was that huge numbers of the hundreds of patients who came into Casualty each day were, in fact, emotionally – rather than physically – disturbed.

I've referred earlier to the shock of finding out that so many of my first patients turned out to have nervous and not physical illnesses. In Casualty, it was even more dramatically clear that many of humanity's ailments are psychological. To my astonishment and (to some extent) distress, I found that patient after patient who came into 'Cas' appeared to be suffering from hysteria – or, at least, some hysterical exaggeration of his or her symptoms.

Well, I expect you doubt that – and I doubted it too, in my first few days in Casualty, when the Cas officers kept talking about how many 'nutters' (I'm afraid that was the word used) they had to deal with. Yet one simple thing that helped to convince me was this.

Time and time again, when a Casualty patient was screaming and yelling for no very obvious reason, one of the qualified doctors would call out dramatically, 'Sister: we shall have to give an injection of Apyrogen!'

This jab would be brought by the nurses with all due ceremony, and rammed into the buttock. And, on nearly every occasion, the patient would immediately get better – cured by the magic injection.

And what was in 'Apyrogen'? *Nothing but water*. Such is the suggestibility of human beings. . . .

*   *   *

A fairly typical case of hysteria was that of The Wild Scotsman.

Mr McX 'collapsed' one morning in the local square, screaming loudly about the pain in his belly and thrashing about with his arms and legs. Simultaneously, he evacuated his bowels into his trousers.

A young policeman who was passing felt understandably sympathetic – especially as Mr McX paused for a moment in his violent contortions and told him that his own son was a copper in Glasgow.

The PC helped Mr McX to another Casualty department, which was located a mile or so down the road from us, and stayed with him while he was examined by the Indian doctor in charge. The doc was *not* impressed by Mr McX's bellowings and writhings, and fairly soon told him to go on his way.

Now the young copper was outraged by this – as was Mr McX – and he decided to bring the gent up to our Casualty for a second opinion.

To say that Mr McX arrived in the department like a Caledonian earthquake is something of an understatement. He burst through the doors with arms flailing, bellowing 'I'm dying! I'm dying! Quick, where's the doctor? Help me! Arrrgh! This terrible pain in my tummy!' Close behind him came the now-frantic policeman.

Mr McX advanced through the department grabbing startled nurses and students and doctors as he went, and imploring them to save him. (At this stage, of course, most of us thought this was a genuine medical emergency.) Among the general chaos, a number of the waiting patients decided to push off, possibly because they were alarmed by his manic demeanour. Or maybe they just didn't like the smell of his trousers.

Eventually we got him into a treatment room, put him on a couch and managed to remove enough of his clothes to permit an examination of his belly – despite the fact that every couple of minutes he kept leaping off the couch and trying to flounder out into the reception area, to shout his thanks at the constable.

Meantime the PC was telling his story to the gastro-enterology registrar, who had happened by – presumably attracted by the whiff of something that reminded him of his particular speciality.

'I brought this gentleman here,' said the copper indignantly, 'because that Indian doctor at the other place treated him so disgracefully!'

'Ah yes,' said the gastroenterology registrar cynically. 'A *brown* doctor.'

My head jerked up in disbelief. I was totally amazed that a young medical man could make such a racist remark.

'That's right,' agreed the policeman. 'One of those immigrants. I reckon he's a disgrace to his profession. I think those blackie doctors should be sent 'ome.'

The gastroenterology registrar nodded agreement. 'We don't think very much of the brown doctors here,' he intoned sententiously. 'This kind of thing is typical of them.'

They carried on in much the same vein for a couple of minutes.

Should I have stepped in and contradicted them? Yes – but it would have taken a braver medical student than me to do so. I just went back into the treatment room and helped with the removal of Mr McX's appalling trousers.

Over the next hour or so, batteries of people came in and examined him, while he continued – in a voice that could be heard all over the department – to shout things like: 'God bless that young policeman! I'm sending his name and number to my son in Glasgow so that he can get proper recognition for saving my life!'

As the morning wore on, it gradually became apparent to every single person who'd examined him that there was nothing at all wrong with him (save, of course, hysteria). A nurse was therefore instructed to produce the magic ampoule of sterile water, and this was duly injected into his bottom.

It had the usual remarkable effect, and in a few minutes his terrible pains vanished completely. I imagine the nurses must have cleaned up his trousers, because shortly thereafter he departed happily for home, apparently eager to tell his family and friends about how the doctors had saved his life. The young copper went back to his beat, and Casualty returned to relative peace and quiet.

As for the racist registrar, he is now a professor of psychiatry.

*   *   *

Now, I'm sure that most of you readers out there will find it hard to accept that a very high percentage of the people who pass through a busy Casualty department are emotionally – rather than physically – ill. But I'm afraid it's true: if you don't believe me, ask any doctor.

For human beings are wonderfully suggestible creatures. We worry about something and before very long, our hearts start to pound, or we get breathless, or we get pains in our stomachs or chests.

These symptoms are *not* imaginary, but they ARE caused by emotional stress and tension – which make odd muscles tighten up (so creating pain), or odd hormones go chasing round the body (so causing palpitations or flushing or a feeling that you're about to die).

The doctors who'd been training us over the last couple of years had taught us to recognise a whole batch of patients' symptoms which, so they said, could as a rule be safely discounted, because they just indicated that the patient was (and I quote) 'rather neurotic'.

They included:

'funny feelings' almost *anywhere* in your body;

tightening (or a sensation of a lump) in your throat;

being aware of your heart thumping in your chest;

having a pain that's 'not *really* a pain, you know, doctor. . . .';

almost any symptom *written on a piece of paper which the patient brings into the consulting room with him.* . . .

In later years – long after I'd qualified – I eventually realised two things:

(i) that perfectly reasonable, 'non-neurotic' people frequently have those sort of symptoms when they're overworked or under great stress;

(ii) that, occasionally, the symptoms which we'd been taught to discount really *did* mean serious physical trouble.

But as medical students of twenty-two, we found it easy to accept what the Casualty officers told us: that Mr X with the very vague pain in his chest was a 'nutter'; Miss Y who'd had fourteen X-rays for a non-existent lump in her throat was really suffering from a phobia about cancer; and that Mrs Z with the queer flushing turns was just wildly frustrated, and would feel a great deal better if her husband gave her a 'poke' more often.

Now in a lot of these cases, the Casualty officers were dead right, I'm afraid. But there's a great danger in deciding that symptoms of a particular pattern can *always* be dismissed as 'unimportant' or 'meaningless' or 'imaginary'.

For instance, one night at 3 a.m. during the last part of my stint as a student in Casualty, a young doctor who was running the department on his own made one of the classic misjudgements. A middle-aged man struggled in, clutching his chest and complaining of a pain which didn't fit the textbook descriptions of heart attacks or angina.

'You're all right, old chap,' said the weary Casualty officer. 'Just a touch of indigestion – that's what you've got. I should see your doctor some time if I were you. Good-night. And try not to *worry* so much.'

Off went the patient – and promptly dropped dead in the street outside. A massive swelling of the largest artery in his body had burst inside his chest.

*   *   *

One thing Casualty taught me fairly rapidly was the relationship between booze and bloodshed. Every Casualty officer in the land knows that half an hour after pub closing time (especially at a weekend) All Hell Will Break Loose. . . .

At Queen's Cottage Hospital, you could nearly have set your watch by the alcoholic influx which hit us at about 11 p.m. on a Friday or Saturday. First came the fighters: mostly roaring drunk and mostly (thank heavens) suffering from little more than broken noses, knocked out teeth, or three-inch gashes in their faces. They all smelt of a curious mixture of alcohol and blood which, on the rare occasions when I sniff it now, immediately takes me back to the mayhem of those wild nights.

As a Celt myself, I was a bit saddened to find that so many of them were Scots and (especially) Irish. Before I'd started on Casualty, I'd heard one of the consultants make a rather snooty remark about 'all those Irish down in Casualty'. Unfortunately, it turned out to be true: between 11 p.m. and 2 a.m., Casualty was like the banks of the Liffey. English accents were rare (except among the doctors), and cries of 'Ah sure, doctor dear, I won't be after needing any local anaesthetic!' rang out from the cubicles.

One thing I would say for my Irish compatriots: the type of violence they were involved in was hardly ever vicious or cruel. Almost invariably, it was a case of two gentlemen emerging from a pub and deciding to settle their differences with bare fists, but no weapons.

In particular, I remember stitching up a young Irish lad who had had his face split open in several places by the knuckles of a West Indian with whom he'd had a post-pub disagreement. Eyes still filled with the light of battle, he had nothing but generous praise for his opponent, 'Ah, he was a great foighter dat black guy. Sure, we had a grand punch-up, doctor.'

Alas, not all drunken fighters were so pleasant and sporting. Some of the local villains were only too ready to leap off the couch while I was stitching them up – in order to try and resume the contest with the dented gent in the next cubicle. (And if I tried to stop them, they'd thump *me*.) Others vomited over the nurses or swore vilely at them.

Under the circumstances, it was just as well that we seemed to have a permanent presence of large local policemen who had mostly dropped in for a cup of tea with a favourite nurse. (The coppers were very partial to nurses, and sometimes married them; they clearly regarded the Cas girls as being like themselves – people in uniform, doing a grand job.)

I'm glad to say that, despite the fact that whirlwind fights frequently broke out between patients and police, and sometimes between patients and doctors, there was virtually no police brutality. (Admittedly, I did see a little of it a couple of years later, when I was myself a qualified doctor and Casualty officer.) Perhaps because they were on their best behaviour in front of the nurses, the coppers who frequented Casualty in the early 1960s remained remarkably amiable in the face of often-considerable provocation, virtually never resorting to swearing or unnecessary violence – a remarkable contrast with the Psychopathic Policemen's Rugby Team who appear in a later chapter of this book.

The Casualty coppers' only major defect, it seemed to me, was that they found it very hard to deal with the West Indians, who made up a large proportion of the patients – especially on Saturday nights after 'chucking-out time'.

The cops just didn't seem to share the feeling which most of us students had about the black patients: we regarded them as mainly good-natured and good fun, and amazingly full of gratitude for any medical attention we gave them.

Unfortunately, even the nicest policemen seemed to have a tendency to regard them as a potential *threat*, rather than as people who were worth getting to know.

During my time on Casualty, I grew to like the West Indians so much, with their easy sense of humour and their open-spirited natures, that I began to think seriously about spending part of my career working with them. Largely as a result of those friendly encounters with bruised and bleeding West Indians in Casualty, I landed up, a few years later, in practice in Jamaica.

You'll notice that I said 'bruised and bleeding,' and it's true that many of the Jamaicans, Barbajans and Trinidadians came in because they'd been in a fight. But all that time, it was mostly pretty minor domestic skirmishing (like, for instance, a man being belted by his missus after one glass too many of rum). Vicious crime and mugging were still very rare among the extremely law-abiding black population of London in the 1960s. Nor was there any indication that the charming West Indian children who often accompanied their parents into Casualty might grow up to be permanently unemployed and resentful of the society which denied them work.

However, there was one obvious and worrying cloud on the horizon. All too frequently, some small, respectable West Indian would be brought in with his face badly bashed. As I stitched him up, I'd ask what had happened and he'd say something like, 'Four guys jumped out, doc, and said they were gonna beat me up *because I am black*.'

The seeds of terrible trouble had already been sown in Black London. Unfortunately, there was no one of goodwill who seemed to have the drive and the ability to try to put things right before it was too late.

*   *   *

Late at night, soon after the fighters, came the road accidents. Britain still had no breathalyser law, but two hours in a Casualty department on a Friday, Saturday or

Sunday night would have convinced almost anybody of the desperate need for one.

In the earlier part of the evening, we might have had a few relatively peaceful hours – enlivened towards the end by a couple of alcoholic punch-ups swirling in through the entrance and sweeping up nurses, doctors and students, much as whirlwinds sweep up leaves.

Then it would happen: the clang of the first ambulance bell of the night. In through the double doors would pour hordes of (mainly) young people – bewildered, hysterical, vomiting, bleeding and sometimes plain dead. They nearly all smelled of booze – except for those who'd been the innocent victims of someone else's inebriated driving.

Some of them had their chests stove in, others had eyes hanging out on their faces, some had their feet pointing backwards instead of forwards – and a tragic few had sustained brain damage that would leave them as 'vegetables' for the rest of their lives. I suppose their average age was about twenty-one or twenty-two – the same as ours.

Daunting? Not really. After a few weeks of this I felt extremely happy that I knew how to play my part in helping to sort out these disasters. It became almost second nature to latch on to some task that needed doing desperately but was within my capabilities. If the qualified doctors and the sister were up to their ears in trouble and blood, trying to save the lives of a couple of people whose legs were half ripped off, it seemed no great problem to pick somebody who was less seriously injured (but who might have a few fractures and have suffered some blood loss), calm him down, take blood for grouping and cross-matching, set up a drip – and then tell the qualified docs that one patient at least was 'under control'.

As you'll probably gather from the above, I had (like many of the medical students) come to love Casualty, regarding it not as a fearful place, but a fascinating one, where rich experience was to be gained. Especially after the pubs turned out.

Indeed, during my last two years as a student I made a regular habit of calling in there for a couple of hours after the evening's study was over, to see what could be learned and what could be done. In fact, myself and one or two of my friends made a slightly bizarre practice of dropping in at midnight or 1 a.m. after attending a dinner or a ball (that is, assuming we were sober).

Surprisingly enough, the patients seemed to be quite pleased to be examined by young gentlemen who were wearing dinner jackets and also sporting carnations in their buttonholes! I suppose many of them felt reassured that they were clearly being treated by very posh docs indeed. . . .

*   *   *

The other factor which made us spend so much voluntary time in Casualty in the middle of the night was, of course, the presence of the nurses – who, in the quieter hours, dispensed cocoa and elementary gynaecology lessons in a most comforting fashion.

These Casualty girls were quick-thinking, intelligent, courteous and utterly reliable in time of emergency. If somebody was bleeding to death, you knew with absolute certainty that one of them would be right behind you, ready to press the life-saving instrument or dressing into your hand. Great girls!

For sociological reasons, I suppose it's worth recording that they had a far freer attitude to sex than most young women of the early 1960s. Maybe it was the constant contact with high drama and with life or death situations. Maybe it was the fact that, unlike so many girls of the long post-war era, they were *totally* familiar with the male body – they'd seen and indeed handled so many undressed men that they weren't remotely shocked by the organ which was so *very* frightening to many women of their generation (and, I assure you, to a few women of today's generation).

Whatever the reason, they were often very free with

restorative midnight kisses, and very obliging about relieving a favoured young medic's frustrations at four o'clock in the morning, or agreeing to spend a weekend in Sussex under the name of 'Jones' or 'Brown' – equipped with that now-defunct badge of 'respectability': a Woolworths' wedding ring (price two and sixpence).

*   *   *

As the years of studentship went by, I'd spent so much time in Casualty that I began to feel ready to cope with anything (well, almost). The sound of an ambulance bell had an almost Pavlovian effect on me, sending me pelting towards Casualty to see if I could help. Flowing blood, instead of being repulsive, stimulated me to *do* something about it – fast.

Big-headedly, I felt totally assured that I could now stop torrential bleeding (by knowing how and where to exert pressure), or save the life of a suicide (by washing out his stomach), or re-start a heart (at that time, some of us even carried a scalpel at all times, in case we needed to open a heart-attack victim's chest in the street). I was probably totally oblivious of the fact that I had no idea at all of how to deliver a baby – or, indeed, of how to communicate with the average patient.

Still, Casualty had been a wonderful training, and had given me immense confidence in myself. You may well think, from what you've read, that at times we were given far too much responsibility for boys of such tender years – and I suppose you'd be right.

Certainly, I do remember exceeding my own limits while helping out in Cas one night when dozens of people were being admitted after a series of bad road accidents.

Although I was still only a senior student, I found myself being left to stitch up the criss-crossed face of a pretty Irish girl whose forehead, cheeks and nose had been very badly slashed by glass.

She was a brave young woman, but it was a two-hour job

and towards the end she began to get understandably worried about whether her face was going to be ruined for ever. One of my friends tried to reassure her that I was doing a good job (with the delicate little stitches that I now used).

But about then, her boy-friend arrived in Casualty, and could be heard talking angrily outside.

'Why's he so cross?' I asked her.

'Ah,' she said with simple certainty, 'he'll be looking for the fella who was driving the other car – to murder him.'

'Oh,' I said.

'And,' she added sweetly, 'he'll probably murder you too if you make a mess of me face. . . .'

It was at that point I began to realise that what this young lady really needed was a plastic surgeon, and *not* a medical student.

How did her face finish up when it had healed? Once again, because of the vast volume of human 'traffic', I have no way of knowing – though I think and hope that her beauty wasn't ruined by my efforts. (Certainly, her boy-friend didn't come round and beat me up.)

So, if you're carted into an accident and emergency department with a badly smashed-up face, always DEMAND that you're stitched up by a qualified surgeon (preferably a *plastic* surgeon if one is available), and don't let a medical student try his hand at running repairs.

Oddly enough, a few years ago my wife (Christine Webber, the television presenter) was badly slashed in a road accident. Since she's in show business, this was a potential tragedy for her – especially as the young house surgeon who began by trying to repair her arm did so with crude, unsophisticated stitches which have left her with scars to this day.

Fortunately, before he could progress to her face, she came round a bit and began to insist determinedly on seeing someone better qualified. After a certain inevitable delay, a clever Indian plastic surgeon was summoned – and he succeeded in saving her appearance by the skill of his suturing.

*   *   *

So, the long days and nights on Casualty had been a wonderful confidence-builder. They'd also been (though we didn't know it) a good preliminary training for general practice – which, like Casualty, mixes up really serious conditions with a great mass of trivia.

Indeed, one of the biggest problems for Casualty departments (then as now) was trying to induce people with trivial complaints to go away so that we could get on with treating the real emergencies. As we battled on, trying to cope with patients who had badly bleeding ulcers, serious burns, or major psychiatric crises, we always seemed to have to deal at the same time with a long, long queue of people who had wandered in because of piles or headaches or toothache or bad colds.

My friend Ben – a student in the year younger than me – invented a quite brilliant way of 'clearing' the Casualty queue. It was this.

One morning, dressed in surgeon's apron, cap and mask, he called a young man from the head of the queue into the treatment room. Unknown to the rest of the patients, the young gent was actually a 'plant' – a fellow medical student.

About two minutes went by; then Ben came bursting out of the treatment room doors, dragging a trolley behind him. On it was the supine body of his friend with a sheet drawn over his face.

Ben pulled it briskly up the corridor past the horrified queue, and took it round the nearest corner. A moment later he returned, clapped his gloved hands together, and addressed the astounded punters.

'Right,' he said. *'Next!'*

As you may imagine, most of the queue disappeared out the door like Chinese whippets. . . .

9

FROM EARS TO MATERNITY

SO THERE I was in my fourth year as a medical student,
aged twenty-two and with a modest knowledge of internal
medicine, general surgery, Casualty – and not much else.

But now came the time when we had to find out about
some of the dozens of other specialities with which
medicine is littered: for instance, ear, nose and throat,
eyes, urology, and of course gynaecology.

In retrospect, it seems as if what we got that year was a
sort of 'passport' allowing us to peer into all available
human orifices and (if possible) to poke our fingers into
them as well.

While that may sound a bit ribald, the fact is that it is of
course a great *privilege* to be allowed to look into somebody's most intimate bits – whether it's down their
windpipe or up their bottoms. Not all of us found it easy to
cope with that privilege.

Beginning with bottoms, let me explain about *that*
particular examination – which I don't think has ever been
clarified to the public in print before! Certainly, when I was
doing health screening sessions a year or two ago, many of
our patients seemed to be completely amazed that we
almost invariably concluded the check-up by sticking a
rather uncomfortable finger up their rear ends.

Why do doctors do it?

Well, first of all it lets you get about four inches into a patient's abdomen – which may be quite helpful if you're trying to sort out the cause of some mysterious pain. But the most important reason is that it can help you to palpate some serious lesion like a tumour of the rectum.

Also, as us medical students soon learned, when you examine a *man* rectally you can, by twiddling your finger round, feel his prostate gland and assess its size and condition. (In some circles, this is practised socially – there's even an oriental musical instrument called the Chinese prostate violin. But I certainly don't propose to go into that here. Try *Grove's Dictionary of Music*.)

It wasn't easy to start doing rectal examinations at medical school. We were embarrassed; the patients were embarrassed; and sometimes even the senior doctors were a bit embarrassed. The previous year, when I'd passed through Dr Morecambe's Medical Firm, he'd made a point of sending all the students out of the room when he did a rectal (which wasn't often).

I actually thought he was quite right to spare the patients' blushes in this way. However, my closest friend Michael Beall – who was the most brilliant student of our time – raged at this 'over-sensitivity', and thought it was quite ridiculous that such a fuss should be made about 'what ought to be a routine examination.' I disagreed.

Yet . . . in a way, I can see what he was driving at now. Because of embarrassment and pressure of time, doctors don't do nearly enough rectal examinations. (A recent study of a large group of patients with bowel symptoms showed that half of them had never been examined *per rectum* by their GPs.)

Michael, incisive, clever and determined, soon found a way of proving his point. Whenever left alone with a patient, instead of indulging in amiable chit-chat, he'd always seize the opportunity to do a quick rectal. (And *no* – he definitely wasn't gay. . . .)

I don't quite know how this policy went down with the

poor old patients, but within a few weeks it produced a startling result. Left in a cubicle for five minutes with a man who had some innocuous bump on his skin, Michael persuaded him to let his backside be examined – and discovered an early carcinoma of the rectum. It had thus far produced no symptoms at all.

By doing this, Michael almost certainly saved the man's life – and, of course, at the same time he established his reputation as a 'high flyer'.

Gradually, we got a bit better (and, I hope, a bit more gentle and considerate) about carrying out rectal exams, though I suspect that one or two boys qualified without ever doing more than half a dozen. We also learned to insert little proctoscopes (instruments for looking at piles), and were even taught how to put in those extraordinarily long telescope-like instruments which enabled us to see a foot or so up a person's bowel: it was a bizarre sensation indeed to look so far inside the human body.

It was also quite surprising to find that (unless you were unlucky) the large bowel was actually a reasonably clean-looking tube – considering what passed through it every day. Not for the first time, I thought how strange it was that the human body could operate so efficiently and neatly, day in, day out, year after year, with very little need for the intervention of either physicians or surgeons.

Alas, these high-flown thoughts were often interrupted by the sigmoidoscope's habit of blasting back vast and noisy gusts of wind in one's face! Perhaps it's not surprising that virtually all doctors find that in order to cope with the sights and sounds and smells of rectal medicine, they have to resort to a degree of scatological humour.

That fact will doubtless upset you if you're of a refined and delicate nature, but there it is. You will probably be appalled to know that almost any doctors' meeting can be reduced to laughter by a *double entendre* concerning the abbreviation 'PR' – which to us means not 'public relations', but '*per rectum*'.

And I expect that you'll be disgusted to learn that not long ago, a medical journal offered as a prize to its readers a silver-plated proctoscope engraved with the words 'For looking up old friends – and enlarging the circle of your acquaintances.'

But I do assure you: in a very stressful profession, laughter makes everything (from backsides and excrement to carcinoma and death) emotionally bearable.

Well, just about.

*   *   *

So, we moved on to gynaecology – and to the problems of the unique and intimate physical examination associated with *that* particular speciality (more of which in a moment).

'Gynae', I found, was an absolutely riveting subject. Here were sick women coming in with problems for which, quite often, there was actually a straightforward *cure* – something that all too often hadn't been the case in the general medicine and general surgery wards.

I liked the patients, and I liked the shy way in which they were willing to confide their worries (often for the very first time) to an equally shy boy in a white coat. Any fool can see that this experience was a forewarning of the fact that one day I would become Britain's most notorious (and disreputable) 'agony aunt'.

And indeed, any Freudian-trained fool can see that the satisfaction I found in seeing these women being helped and cured in the gynaecology department was not unconnected with the past despair I had felt at my own mother's long and incurable illnesses. But that's not unusual: a considerable number of gynaecologists have had childhoods which were coloured by severe maternal illness, and so have grown up with a deep emotional need to help women.

However, nearly all gynaecologists are also *surgeons* – which means that in many cases, their personalities have the characteristic surgical drive and cheek and abrasiveness which I've described in the last chapter but one.

I've found that many of them are very kind men (unfortunately, the great majority of gynaecologists are still male); but their surgical hauteur and aloofness do quite often make them far less capable than they imagine in communicating with their women patients. For instance, one of my dearest friends, who is a gynaecologist, once said to me in front of a crippled patient with a bent spine, 'This lady presents the typical Hunchback of Notre Dame picture. . . .'

He still has no idea of what he did that day to that woman's confidence.

However, we were fortunate at Queen's Cottage Hospital in having three of the country's best – and, I think kindest – gynaecologists in charge of the department.

All three were knighted (you can see what posh circles us students were moving in!), and in my view deservedly so. They were all good surgeons, but also intelligent, innovative men who were exploring new areas of treatment with hormones instead of surgery. One of them was so 'advanced' in thought that he actually gave us a lecture on the Dutch cap – almost the only teaching on contraception which we had in all our five years' training.

More importantly, all three of them set us an excellent example by being basically *nice* to their patients, even if they were also sometimes a trifle remote. I expect they felt that with their impressive Royal Connections, they were entitled to be just a *teeny* bit detached, especially on days when they were visiting the Palace.

The most famous of them was the legendary Sir James Ring, who had delivered most of the Royal babies of recent years. He struck me as a quiet, considerate man, and his lady patients regarded him as 'a real gent'. He also seemed to be totally calm, and unfazed by anything.

But many years later, my mother-in-law pointed out something that I'd missed. She told me that she'd been examined by him in those days of the early 60s – and that she had been a trifle discomfited by the fact that during the entire vaginal examination, the poor man had been afflicted by a disabling facial tic.

It was true: but we students had hardly noticed it. So like some (or most) of us, he too had presumably been 'playing a part', and struggling to control very human worries and tensions.

* * *

That brings me to the inevitable subject of *vaginal examination*: again, something which I've never seen discussed frankly in the public prints!

Most female readers already know what it's like to be on the receiving of an 'internal'.

But I'd better tell male readers that for a woman an examination *per vaginam* can easily be a rather degrading experience. Many women feel very threatened by it. And if the doctor isn't very good at it, or if the patient is tense (both situations being common), it can be uncomfortable or even painful.

A lot of blokes – like a few of the sillier young medical students of my day – think that a woman must *enjoy* a vaginal examination ('They love every minute of it, old boy!'). In reality, she may well dread it.

Anyway, in Sir James' Gynaecology Out-patient Department, we were faced with doing our first 'PVs' on patients.

Sir James – very decently by the standards of those days – always asked the woman's permission with some courtesy before letting a student examine her vaginally. And he only (only!) allowed *four* of us medics do a PV on each patient. If you think that four is far too many, I agree that you have a formidable case – yet there were about sixteen students on the Gynae Firm, so who were they going to learn on?

Perhaps one cynical answer (by today's permissive standards) is 'on their girl-friends'. But in those very early 1960s, we had medical students who were not only virgins, but who had never been out with a woman in their lives!

So, imagine a number of twenty-one- or twenty-two-year-old boys being told to don an ill-fitting rubber glove, lubricate it with surgical jelly and then – under the gaze of the rest of the firm – insert two fingers up some poor worried lady's vagina.

For several of the lads, it was clearly very embarrassing – and it was noticeable that one or two of them rarely turned up again at gynac out-patients, preferring to head for the snooker table or the poker school instead.

What this meant, of course, was that they eventually qualified as doctors having done hardly any vaginal examinations at all (except the obligatory ones during the last part of childbirth – please see the next chapter). You might find that quite unbelievable: yet the fact is that a study published in the *British Medical Journal* in 1971 showed that at that period, a third of general practitioners didn't even possess the equipment to do a vaginal examination.

What an appalling state of affairs! Women who went to these doctors with a gynaecological complaint were told to 'put up with it', or had something prescribed for them totally 'blind' – or else were just referred by their GPs to a hospital gynaecologist, perhaps having to wait four or five months to see him.

During my years in general practice, I'm glad to say that I watched things improve very greatly. But far into the 1970s, I still found myself again and again going into inner city general practices where it was obvious from the lack of equipment that the GP *never* did a vaginal examination, probably because he was too embarrassed or too frightened – and perhaps because he had never learned the technique as a medical student.

How many patients died of cancer as a result? I don't know – but I am profoundly glad that the standard of most British family doctors is far higher than that these days.

*   *   *

The vaginal examination technique is quite tricky, but if you're blessed with long and reasonably sensitive fingers, it can give you a lot of information about the patient's cervix, womb and ovaries, and about the bits nearby which you can feel through her vaginal wall. (Alas, one of the sad consequences of learning to examine vaginally with a degree of skill is that for the rest of your life, you will *never* be able to make love to a woman without being aware of whether she is constipated or not. . . .)

I was very lucky in that I found the PV reasonably easy to do, partly (to be frank) because of my previous very happy love-life. The vagina didn't strike me as a threatening organ – which was clearly just how it struck several of my colleagues. Their unease about 'the cunt' came out very strongly in some of the beery songs and jokes with which they helped to celebrate after our rugby matches.

Furthermore, I was pleased that, like several of my friends, I found that I could get the patients to relax and *talk* while they were being examined. Years later, research by members of the Institute of Psycho-Sexual Medicine showed that when a woman is having an 'internal', there's often a rather surprising 'moment of truth', in which she's willing to reveal what is *really* worrying her about her sex organs – or, very often, her sex life.

*   *   *

Speaking of sex, the question which some readers will be itching to ask is this: Wasn't all this vaginal examination in the out-patients department a sexual 'turn-on' for the male students?

And the answer is: I don't think so. As I've already implied, some of the boys were actually very 'turned off' by this alarming contact with the personal parts of women. For the rest of us, I don't believe the situation was the least bit erotic, still less romantic – though I may be wrong.

For a start, gynae out-patients was – to be brutally frank – always a trifle smelly, despite sister's efforts with the

deodorant bottle. Much more importantly, my closest
friends and I seemed to be totally concerned with:

(a) improving our own clinical skills;
(b) trying to make a good impression on the consultant;
(c) trying to find out what was wrong with these poor
    bloody (often *literally* bloody) women, so as to help
    them.

We had no time or energy left for getting erections.

*   *   *

So what *was* wrong with these women?

The common conditions which brought people to the
gynaecology department included vaginal infections like
thrush and trichomonas – which caused intensely irritating
and embarrassing inflammation of the vagina.

I remember one of the first women who came in. Like so
many others, she'd been struggling with her infection (with
its accompanying yellow discharge) for many months,
believing that she 'had to put up with it'. Any attempt at
physical love during that time must have been appallingly
painful for her; work must have been a nightmare too, and
she was clearly at her wits' end.

But Sir James put her at her ease, examined her, then
showed us how the correct diagnosis could be made very
easily. He took a drop of moisture from her vagina, put it
under the little microscope which he kept in the out-
patients department, and then invited us to have a look.

There was the root of all the pain and trouble: the
infuriating little bug called 'trichomonas', tiny and transparent, threshing around on the glass slide. It's the cause of
quite a lot of human misery, sometimes even contributing
to marital breakdown, and yet it can so easily be wiped out
of a woman's vagina with the correct medication – once the
right diagnosis has been made.

What else did we see?

There were countless women whose lives were being
made hell by periods: for instance, periods that caused

them intense pain, or periods that flooded and flooded, soaking their clothing and defying all attempts – with towel and tampon – to keep the blood in check.

Again, many of the women had battled on for months or years, often assured by mothers, grandmothers or doctors that it was 'just woman's lot, dear.'

Not *all* of them could be helped at that time in the early 1960s, but a high proportion were made better, either by judicious surgery or the use of the new hormones.

Finally, there were the cancer cases. What struck me about them (apart from the sadness and waste) was the enormous opportunity for *early detection* of gynaecological cancer. Let me give you two examples.

Mrs Fife turned up at the hospital complaining of bleeding between the periods, especially after sex. She'd first noticed it a year or so before, but had done nothing about it for several months. She hadn't realised it was anything to bother about. When she'd eventually gone to her doctor, she had (quite frankly) been fobbed off by him. Several more months passed before he'd sent her to the hospital.

Now . . . well, it was all too clear from examining her that her cancer of the cervix had gone far too far. The consultant would arrange some palliative radiotherapy, but her relatively young life would very soon be over.

In contrast, Mrs Matthews had gone to her GP after only one post-intercourse bleed. An alert man, he had got her to the clinic very fast – and the result was that a fairly minor operation removed her early cancer, and saved her life.

It was a startling example of what could be done by early detection, and there were plenty of others. For instance, I slowly grasped that *if only all women had smear tests, virtually none of them would die of carcinoma of the cervix*.

Alas, in Britain today that lesson *still* hasn't been widely learned. Two thousand women still die of that disease, and the vast majority of them have never had a smear test at all.

Similarly, my friend Michael Beall – the bloke who would one day be a consultant at the Mayo Clinic – pointed out to me that hardly any of the women patients realised that bleeding *after the menopause* was a potentially serious symptom, since it so often indicated another cancer – namely cancer of the womb lining.

Michael had a typically clever (if slightly impractical) scheme to wipe out all the thousands of deaths from that type of carcinoma.

'Put an observer behind a peephole in every ladies' toilet,' he said.

'Wot for?' said I.

'As soon as the observer sees a woman over fifty slipping a coin in the sanitary towel machine, he'll nip out and invite her to come up to the hospital right away to be tested for cancer. Think of all the lives it'll save!'

It did occur to me that there might be a slightly simpler way of increasing public awareness of the early signs of gynaecological cancer: *write about it in women's magazines*.

*   *   *

In the latter part of that year, we moved on to other things, such as peering into people's eyes, and their ears and noses and throats.

'ENT' was a delightful subject, taught by three chaps in superbly-cut suits. Their every gesture and every intonation spelt Harley Street – though only one of them had so far got a knighthood. Like the others, he seemed to have founded his fortune on taking out prodigious numbers of tonsils.

He was a surgeon with an incredibly dominating personality (surprise! surprise!), a man who had pioneered a wonderful new operation – carried out with the aid of a microscope – which cured a common form of middle-aged deafness. Had Beethoven still been alive, Sir Montague could almost certainly have cured him. Or so he said.

To us, he was especially revered because . . . He Had Operated On Elizabeth Taylor.

Saying this breaks no medical confidences, since the facts were fully aired in the popular press – and, alas, the courts – at the time.

Liz Taylor had gone down with one of her many disastrous illnesses. This time it had been staphylococcal pneumonia, and her life had been in very great danger. Sir Montague saved it – by doing a tracheotomy, the operation in which you cut straight into the windpipe through the front of the neck.

Unfortunately, Liz didn't appear to be all that grateful, and later took unsuccessful legal action against him.

Why? Well, for some reason that world-famous and much-respected man had chosen to do the emergency operation through a *vertical* incision in the skin of the front of her neck, instead of the horizontal one used by most modern surgeons.

The vertical incision is much more likely to cause a visible scar, and that's what Liz was left with. You can see it every time they show *Cleopatra* on TV.

*   *   *

So that was oto-rhino-laryngology (which is the posh name for ENT). We had picked up a working knowledge of it in a few weeks (by which time I was convinced that most children were having their tonsils taken out *completely* unnecessarily), and by then it was time to move on – to every other '-ology' you could think of.

We ploughed manfully through (to name but a few) dermatology, urology, microbiology, haematology, chemical pathology, venereology, histology and neurology (the most amazing thing about that particular subject was that the very brilliant consultant in charge hadn't actually been seen on the wards for the last twenty years!).

Dozens upon dozens of subjects had to be crammed in. However, there was absolutely no teaching on general practice, which was quite crazy, of course, bearing in mind that so many of us would be GPs. Nor was there anything on geriatrics.

These days, I'm glad to say, medical students *are* taught about general practice. But according to my current General Medical Council reports, even now hardly any of them are taught any geriatrics. Potty.

You can see that the pressure on us was intense. When it came to studying ophthalmology (eyes), we discovered with relief that, for some mad reason, we would *not* be examined on this subject in Finals.

So, several of us just decided not to learn anything about the eyes at all! I'm appalled to say that almost everything I now know about this important subject was acquired soon *after* I qualified as a doctor.

If you feel like criticizing, then I ask you to consider the truly vast amount of information that we were being asked to absorb in just a few short years before our Final exams. For instance, during my six months on Mr W.-B.'s Surgical Firm, I'd tried to commit to memory (among much else) the greater part of Bailey and Love's fact-packed *Short Practice of Surgery*. It still stands on my bookshelf, and it is 1,389 large pages long.

We only achieved these quite massive feats of learning through adopting a fairly workaholic pace which for many of us would, unfortunately, be continued during the rest of our lives.

After a quite long day's slog on the wards or in the operating theatre, most of us would get down to the books and our notes, and study far into the night. There was really little other choice if you wanted to pass Finals.

In my case, I spent evening after evening with Michael Beall, or some other like-minded medic, making long lists of diseases and symptoms, testing each other with difficult case histories, and pitting our memories against each other in contests to see who could remember great long slabs of textbook. Even if we adjourned to the pub, we still continued to talk and talk and talk about medicine, and teach each other facts that we'd picked up during the day. (However, studying in the local boozer is *not* something I'd recommend to any student of anything: by the time you're on your second pint, the learning capacity of your brain is already worth just about nil!)

It was, quite honestly, a tough and stressful life. But we'd acquired a remarkable amount of knowledge in a pretty short period. However, now it was time to go on to obstetrics; I looked forward with immense pleasure to finding out about the miraculous business of childbirth.

But before I tell you about obstetrics, one final word about gynaecology and this vexed business of how students learn (or don't learn) to do a vaginal examination. During the period when I was writing this book (1988–89), Mrs Jean Robinson – a non-medical member of the General Medical Council – started a campaign against the current practice of allowing medical students to do PVs on women patients *who are unconscious under anaesthesia*. The GMC didn't think there was anything wrong with this.

I mentioned that fact in one of my agony aunt columns – and was promptly inundated with letters from women who were very, very angry indeed at having been examined by students while unconscious. 'I felt *violated*,' wrote one reader.

However, among the letters was a most fascinating one from a Dutch lady. It explained that a medical school in Holland has set up a completely new programme for dealing with the problems of giving medical students experience of intimate examinations. It works like this:

When they are studying gynaecology and obstetrics, every medical student has to get on the couch and have his or her intimate bits felt by the rest of the class! It sounded extraordinary to me, and my first thought was that the girl students would be less than enthusiastic about having to submit to vaginal examination by all the boys. But, according to my correspondent, in solid, practical old

Holland it all works out fine – especially as the women students actually outnumber the men. Doubtless they could get their revenge if any of the male students were careless or rough. . . .

All of which reminds me of a proposal which is said to have been put forward not long ago by an American woman MD. She advocated that in order to let male medical students know what women patients go through, the following procedure should be made compulsory during the study of gynaecology and obstetrics:

The male medical student should be shown into a cold examination room and told abruptly to remove all his clothes below the waist. He should then be placed on a chilly couch with his legs up in 'stirrups'. After that, he should be left completely alone in fearful contemplation for twenty minutes.

At the end of that time, a group of grim-looking women in white coats should stride in, walk up to him – and squeeze his balls with very chilly hands.

Then they should walk straight out again – without saying a word.

Touché, ma'am – *touché*.

10

BABIES, BABIES

BABIES FIGURED FAIRLY prominently in our fourth year of medicine. And I don't just mean the babies which we were about to start delivering on the wards. Alas, two of the boys in our year (both of whom were called Fred) managed to sire babies by student nurses almost simultaneously – and married them just in the nick of time.

I'm afraid our general reaction to this double disaster was hilarity, combined with a feeling of intense relief that it wasn't *us* who'd been caught.

But hilarity turned to sadness shortly afterwards when, perhaps unwisely, one of the Freds went out for a night with three other lads. On the way home, the car crashed, killing all four of them. So, a young nurse was left with a fatherless baby and no career.

Despite this tragedy, death was a thing that still seemed quite remote to me. That may seem odd, considering that I'd spent two years dissecting dead people. Also, many of the patients who I'd known on the wards had died overnight – when I wasn't there. And I'd examined patients brought newly-dead into Casualty.

But like most of the rest of the students, I suppose, I'd never *seen* anyone pass through the gate of death. Like birth, it was something a bit beyond my comprehension.

And, of course, that old nagging thought bothered me: could I cope with it?

*   *   *

Before long it happened. A friend of mine and I had just gone into residence to start our midwifery course. No expectant mums were ready to 'pop' on the first evening, so there was little to do except study and drink coffee.

Late that first night, Douglas and I wandered into the nearby Casualty department and found ourselves being roped in to help look after an old lady who'd been brought in unconscious, having fallen downstairs and badly injured her head.

The neurosurgical registrar, a reliable, greying man in his late thirties, told us what to do and we did it. We placed her in the 'recovery position' on a trolley, made sure her airway was clear, set up a chart on which to record her vital signs, took her blood pressure and checked her pupils, and then swept her off to the X-ray department. Twenty minutes later, we were back in the Casualty ward with the films. They showed that she had a massive skull fracture. And the symptoms which we were plotting on our chart showed that she was bleeding prodigiously inside her brain.

What was to be done? The registrar examined her again, and shook his head gently. 'We won't be able to save her,' he murmured.

Douglas and I kept a watch on her for the next hour or so as the life seeped inexorably away. I can still see the sweet, fragile, eighty-year-old head, with the white, damp curls sticking to it. (Funny how often the hair sticks to the skull in somebody who's ill.)

After a while, she just quietly died. There was no pain or struggle; she merely slipped away gradually, until the heart and the breathing stopped.

I felt no fear or distress, but perhaps a certain sense of privilege at having been there, and having helped to make sure she was comfortable at her passing. I was glad too that it had been pain-free – like most of the many deaths I've witnessed since then. Death is not usually painful.

The registrar came back, officially pronounced her dead, and sent for the porters to take her away.

Then (wise man) he took us round to the resident quarters for a very late cuppa and a chat about what we'd seen. I wish there had been more like him.

Firmly but gently, he dealt with the question that was now in our minds: couldn't we have done something to save her?

'No – there comes a time when enough is enough. When somebody's nearly reached the end of their life and is weak and frail, you don't subject them to massive heroic operations. You let them go in peace.'

It wasn't bad advice, and I tried to remember it from then on. You may think that what the registrar said was arrogant; you may believe (as I had until that night) that doctors fight until the very last gasp to keep life going at all costs and in all circumstances. I'm afraid we don't.

Of course, it's very important that doctors shouldn't allow themselves to become careless or disrespectful of life (more of that later in this chapter when we get back to the question of babies). Those attitudes can easily creep into a profession that is already more than a little inclined toward playing God.

For instance, there was an episode a few years ago when it was found that a considerable number of patients at a hospital had had their notes stamped, on doctor's orders, with the letters 'NFR'.

This meant 'Not For Resuscitation' – in other words 'to be allowed to die'. Quite understandably, the relatives of some of these people were less than pleased at such a sweeping and seemingly callous consignment of their loved ones to the scrap-heap.

On the other hand, many years after qualifying, I remember being impressed by the thoughtful words of a Jamaican nurse who was looking after a terminally ill patient – a woman who had been hauled back from the brink of death *against her will* time and time again.

Said the nurse, 'It's like you want to go to sleep real bad – and someone just keeps on and on shakin' your shoulder and wakin' you up.'

I think she was right. I know this is a difficult area of ethics, but I hope that when my own time comes, no one will be daft enough to keep shakin' my shoulder and wakin' me up. . . .

*   *   *

I mentioned Douglas, the friend with whom I started the midwifery course. He was from East Africa: very tall, very black, very handsome, and very bright.

But he found coping with the ethical and emotional demands of medicine extremely difficult. Like one or two others in my year, he had a brilliant early career as a student, but just seemed to fall apart as the medical course progressed. He qualified years late, and with considerable difficulty and much emotional distress.

In fact, breakdowns like his were quite common among the medics, though no one in our stiff-upper-lip environment seemed very willing to acknowledge the fact.

A recent American study shows that up to a quarter of US medical students have serious symptoms of depression during the latter part of their course. In late 1988, the *Journal of the American Medical Association* said that the incidence of depressive illness in medical students was 'disturbingly high' – far in excess of that in the rest of the population. That accords very well with my recollections of what happened to my friends under the twin pressures of an enormous study-load *and* the colossal burden of dealing with matters of life and death – plus, of course, the added difficulties of coping with one's own love life.

Among my close friends, I remember particularly Harry Coleman (all these names are changed, of course), who helped me treat numerous overdoses in Casualty – and who was eventually brought in unconscious and full of barbiturates himself. Like many attempted suicides, he recovered well, and eventually made a great success of his career.

I remember also Jim Harwood – always cheerful and laughing, yet secretly desperate that once a week someone would see him creeping along the corridor that led to the psychiatrist's consulting room. (He only told me about that many years later, when he'd become a surgeon.)

And, most of all, I remember nice old Frank Macgregor – funny, witty, a great companion and for several years my closest mate. Overwhelmed by it all (and also totally unable to reconcile his strict Catholicism with his intense desire to take nurses to bed), he cracked up completely – and was found wandering in a nearby park, trying to heal a dead sparrow with his bare hands. He eventually recovered, qualified and became a good and useful doctor. But to this day I deeply regret that I didn't do more to see the trouble coming and to help him when he was breaking down.

Some very hard, tough boys seemed to get through the course without a qualm. Others (too many) got by with the help of heavy drinking – a path I very nearly went along myself. There but for the Price of Beer. . . .

I spent most of the 1980s sitting on the General Medical Council committee that deals with sick doctors, and I can tell you that the tragic fact is that alcohol is the medical profession's Achilles' heel. Unfortunately, statistics show that we are far more likely than most of the rest of the population to fall victim to drink or drugs. Our suicide rate is also far higher than the rest of humanity's, with women doctors being especially at risk of killing themselves.

So, the stresses of our profession really are very great indeed. My own opinion (for what it's worth) is that those stresses would be much *less* if doctors weren't brought up in the curious tradition of never giving in to your emotions, hardly ever letting your feelings show, and rarely admitting to anyone that you're unsure or bewildered or frightened.

This extraordinary rigidity of outlook was something I encountered repeatedly during the time when I was learning to deliver babies.

* * *

'I thought me heart would burst wit' joy when first I saw a baby born.'

A West Indian midwife said that to me on my first day in the labour ward. And at almost every birth I've seen since then, I've thought of her words.

My first sight of a delivery (in her company) was a joy to *me* too. Until then, I hadn't quite believed that birth was *real*. The idea that a fully-formed baby should come out of that agreeable aperture of a woman was surely all too fantastic: a story just as bizarre as the gooseberry-bush one.

But there I stood, masked and gowned in the delivery room, facing the vulva of a woman in the last stages of labour. The great white mound of her belly loomed in the background, and the dark vulva was expanding and expanding as she groaned and gasped – expanding from a vertical slit into a pear shape, and then into an oval.

Suddenly, I saw that in the middle of the oval was a little tuft of dark hair, on a patch of wrinkled skin no bigger than a coin. And as the patch of skin grew and grew in size, so the vulva enlarged sideways to accommodate it until, unbelievably, the vulval opening was as broad as a saucer.

But that opening was now desperately stretched, and it looked as though its thin, taut edges might split at any moment. It had expanded so much, in fact, that the entrance of the mother's rectum seemed to be stuck on to its lower rim, like a crater at the southern edge of a full moon.

Then suddenly (when it appeared as though the poor over-stretched vulva could cope with no more), the dome of the top of the child's head slipped through it.

'Baby's head is crowned!' yelled the midwife who was standing beside the mother, conducting the delivery. 'Pant like a dog, dear; pant like a dog!' (This, I soon learned, was what midwives always say at the moment of 'crowning'.)

Not much happened for a minute or so, as the mother gave a passable imitation of a breathless labrador. Then, quite abruptly, there was something very like a popping sound – and a small, blue, crumpled face shot out of the vagina. Although I had read all my students' textbooks and knew which way the baby should be facing, nonetheless I was faintly surprised to see that it was *true* that most babies come out looking *backwards*. The little bloke's wee, rubbery nose was more or less poking up his Mum's rear end, which didn't seem to be a very dignified way to start your life.

Be that as it may, it was still a miraculous experience from my point of view. A minute or two later, another remarkable thing happened (just as my textbooks had forecast it would). As the mother's pains returned and her womb began to push down again, the little head started to rotate through ninety degrees until the baby was facing to the *side* rather than directly backwards.

This natural rotation through a right-angle occurred, I realised, because a baby's relatively broad little shoulders can't be born unless they're sideways on. (Think about it: a woman's organ is a *vertical* slit.)

Soon, out popped the small shoulders; the midwife expertly hooked her gloved index fingers under them and began to lift the child gently upwards; a second later, his body, legs and feet were born in a slosh of blood and womb liquid – and it was all over.

The child, still attached to somewhere deep inside the now flat-bellied mother (thanks to that long, knurled cable that ran from his navel), was clearly a boy. Even I knew enough to diagnose that.

No one smacked his bottom (as they do in old novels), but the midwife quickly took a rubber tube and sucked a few gobbets of mucus out of his mouth. Moments later, he gave a loud, wonderful and indignant cry. He was OK.

* * *

It was quite an event; so much so that it has almost wiped out my recollection of the first delivery which I myself conducted, a few days after that.

You may find it surprising that a doctor wouldn't remember 'the first child that he brought into the world.' But having already *seen* a delivery, I found that being the actual deliverer was no big emotional deal – though it definitely afforded me a certain technical satisfaction to know that I managed to get it right.

Two curious facts struck me during those early weeks of obstetrics. Firstly, the old phrase about 'doctors bringing babies into the world' is largely a load of old nonsense. In a *normal* delivery (as opposed to the admittedly very substantial minority which are *abnormal*) the mother and the child virtually do it themselves. The doctor's role during the actual minutes of delivery is mainly confined to reassuring the Mum, telling her how to breathe properly, 'fielding' the baby as it comes out – and refraining from doing anything stupid (like dropping it).

The second fact I noted was this: in the vast majority of cases (at least, in Britain), it's not a doctor who delivers the baby at all – it's a midwife. I was later to discover that occasionally it's the doctor who pockets the fee, while the poor old midwife does the work.

The midwives of Britain (and, indeed, the British Commonwealth) constitute a remarkable, nay, formidable body of women. They often hold views which they will defend to the death – probably *your* death if you disagree with them. Any man who takes them on does so at his peril.

In the labour ward, they regarded us medical students with considerable suspicion – and quite rightly so, too. Not only were we liable to seduce the pretty young pupil midwives who they were training – but, far more important, *we were in direct competition with those same pupil midwives for deliveries*.

You see, a medic has to deliver a set number of babies (usually about twenty) before he's eligible to qualify as a doctor. The pupil midwives also had their 'quota' to fill.

As a result, quite unseemly squabbles often broke out in the labour ward at moments when all should have been tranquil and restful for the mother. I remember one incident in which, as insults flew to and fro across a woman's labouring tum, she interrupted the battle by suddenly interposing, 'Oy! D'you mind not fighting over me? I'm trying to have a baby here!'

*   *   *

The weeks that Douglas and I spent 'in residence', so that we could get to the labour ward quickly, were great fun and full of interest – particularly when I watched the registrars doing the more difficult deliveries: forceps, vacuum extractions and Caesareans.

But they were sometimes horrifying times, too, especially when much-wanted babies died or were stillborn – so much effort on the mother's part, and only tragedy to show for it.

Also, I remember being particularly struck by what seemed to me to be the barbarity of the near-routine use of episiotomy by some doctors – though not usually by the midwives. Episiotomy is the name for the deep cut in the vulva (done with a large pair of scissors) which so many women undergo during the last minute or two of labour.

The idea of it is to widen the passage so that the baby's head can come through. And there's a place for it in some deliveries, because it can prevent a far more jagged and unpleasant *tear*, which may occur when an over-large baby's head virtually explodes through the over-stretched opening.

But episiotomy is a pretty savage thing to do to somebody: if you're a male reader and find that hard to understand, then just imagine how it would be if someone shoved one blade of a pair of scissors a couple of inches up your rectum – and then very sharply snapped the blades together in order to enlarge *your* opening. . . .

Admittedly, many women who have an episiotomy are under the influence of gas, and have had a quick jab of local anaesthetic into the area first (if time permits). But 'local' is of variable effectiveness – and again and again during those weeks, I saw women leap a foot off the bed, screaming in savage pain as the scissors bit into the most intimate and private part of their bodies.

The basic problem was that certain of the registrars took the view that nearly all first-time mothers 'needed' to be cut in this way. I was appalled that so many of the medical students accepted this viewpoint without question as gospel truth, even though there appeared to me to be not the slightest hard *scientific* evidence for it. (It seems to be very common in obstetrics for something to become established practice without any proper scientific trial.)

Sadly, the boys of those days who learned to do virtually routine episiotomies on first-time mums *have carried on doing them*. Until quite recently, in some British hospitals roughly nine out of ten of all mothers had to undergo episiotomy.

But in 1989, *Mother and Baby* magazine (a popular Mums' monthly for which I write) drew the public's attention to the pioneering work of an English midwife who has shown by means of a massive study of 1,000 women and their babies that in most deliveries (not all), there is absolutely *no* point at all in making this deep and painful cut.

Then why on earth have we been doing it as a matter of routine for so long? Because our seniors told us it was a good idea.

* * *

So, the weeks of my spell in obstetric residence passed, and Douglas and I slowly amassed more and more deliveries between us. But between births, we spent long hours in waiting, and studying, and sitting with Mums who were in labour – taking their pulses, listening to the baby's heart through a sort of ear trumpet, doing an occasional vaginal examination to see how things were progressing, and generally trying to cheer the mother up (a most important thing, since labour isn't exactly the easiest thing in the world; unfortunately, far too many labouring Mums are still left in a lonely room with no one to talk to).

We also whiled away the long hours by learning to bottle-feed the babies, a procedure which I enjoyed greatly. There's much satisfaction in wandering into a room full of squalling little pink (or brown or black) bundles, and gradually calming most of them down by either changing their nappies, or else ramming a bottle into the other – and usually noisier – end.

Unfortunately, what we did *not* realise in those days was that cow's milk (which is what ALL bottle feeds are) is actually not too good for many babies, and may indeed be the cause of allergies. All babies who spent a few days in maternity wards at that time inevitably got a hefty dose of cow's milk from passing midwives or medical students. And for many years thereafter, it was quite difficult for a Mum who wanted to *totally* breast-feed her baby to prevent some well-meaning soul from shoving a bottle of cow-juice in his mouth.

Still, my teaching hospital (unlike some others) did actually try hard to *encourage* mothers to breast-feed. This was at a time when there was a widespread belief – fostered, I fear, by the baby milk manufacturers – that a huge proportion of women 'couldn't feed their babies'. It's a ludicrous idea, of course (if it were true, how the heck could the human race have survived so long?), but we students more or less accepted it. It wasn't till years later, when I went to practise in Jamaica – where every single woman breast-fed enthusiastically without a second thought about it – that I realised how completely crazy was the myth that 'some mothers can't breast-feed'.

I have to confess that one of the reasons why I enjoyed tending to the babies in the nursery in the middle of the night was the fact that it gave one such an admirable opportunity for romantic socialising with whichever pupil midwife happened to be in charge. A snatch of dialogue from those heady, milk-scented nights drifts back into my mind:

MEDICAL STUDENT: Nurse, could you just hold this baby for a moment, please?

NURSE: Certainly . . . oooh, isn't he lovely? Look, he's nuzzling into my bosom. Must be instinct, mustn't it?

MEDICAL STUDENT (*standing very close to nurse, who now has both her hands fully occupied*): And who shall blame him, my dear, who shall blame him. . . .

I expect that if you've ploughed on thus far into this book about the tragi-comedy of medicine, you know what I'm going to say next: life on the maternity ward wasn't *all* joyous births and lovely, perfect babies and chatting up nurses at midnight. Yes, as with all of medicine, disaster was always just around the corner.

I saw it first when a baby who I delivered was swept away in a blanket by a midwife before the mother could see it. Amazingly, I myself had scarcely taken in that anything was wrong.

Half an hour later, when I'd sorted out the business of delivering the afterbirth, the obstetric house surgeon (a young man of about twenty-two) came into the room with the child. I must say that despite his inexperience, he probably made the best job he could have done of telling the poor, frightened woman what was wrong.

'Er . . . Mother,' he said. 'I'm glad to say that Baby is perfect in every way – except for his ears.'

He pulled back the shawl and revealed that the wee thing *had no ears at all*. Quite apart from the shock of the child's appearance, it was clear to most people in the room (though perhaps not to the bewildered woman) that the baby would never be able to hear anything.

The mother took it very well, as mothers mostly do when faced with a deformed baby. But it seemed to me surprising that the burden of breaking this awful news had been left to such a young and newly-qualified doctor. (However, still greater responsibilities were apparently left to him, as we'll see in a moment.)

There were, of course, worse tragedies than that on the ward. Mothers came in, laboured hard and bravely – and then gave birth to dead babies. On one occasion, a child was born with no head – a nightmare phenomenon which up till then I'd only seen in a glass pot in the pathology museum. Thank heavens, such things are rarer now, because of routine screening of women for foetal abnormalities in early pregnancy.

But for me, the most shattering experience came one day when Douglas and I were in idle conversation on the ward with a midwife and the house surgeon. He was trying to tell us about a baby who'd been born on another obstetric ward a few days previously. Initially I wasn't paying much attention – and then I heard him say, 'So it had no arms and legs when it was born. Ghastly thing! Well, next morning I walked up there with a syringeful of insulin, and gave it about a hundred units. Felt sure *that'd* kill it.'

I suddenly jerked awake as I realised what he'd said. He went on, oblivious of the shock he'd caused to at least one of his listeners.

'Well, I went up to the ward again next morning, expecting that they'd tell me that the monster child had died. And blow me! There it was, lying in the cot, smiling at me!'

I was too stunned to say anything. I think I may have walked away, because I certainly didn't hear the obstetric house surgeon say whether he'd given this poor, smiling, limbless baby *another* shot of a killer drug.

Rather surprisingly, I don't think I discussed it at all with Douglas when we got back to our quarters. Perhaps it would have been better for him (maybe just possibly he might not have had the breakdown?) if we had been able to talk about such things. . . .

Nor, in case you're wondering, did I report the conversation to anybody in power. There was really no one for us twenty-one-year-olds to report it *to* – and, in any case, for a medical student to have complained about the action taken by a qualified doctor would have been totally unthinkable to any of us.

So, I just kept it to myself, wondering if this was the way that doctors behaved – bumping off babies when they felt that was the right thing to do?

You may wonder how on earth the young house surgeon of about twenty-two or twenty-three felt that he had the moral authority to do such a thing. It was, I think, a manifestation of the 'Doctor-Knows-Best' syndrome. At the time, I remembered the only ethical guidance we'd been given on this subject: one of the most influential consultants in the hospital had delivered a lecture in which he touched briefly on euthanasia; he said pointedly, 'Just make up your own mind what the best course of action is – and do it. And above all, *don't tell anybody what you've done.*'

In other words: 'You know best. . . .'

Had the obstetric house surgeon been given the same advice a couple of years before us? If so, he'd clearly followed the first part of it – but not the second part about keeping it quiet. And did he maybe tell us because he wanted reassurance that what he'd done was right and general among the medical profession?

Please don't get me wrong: I certainly saw no widespread 'doing in' of abnormal babies. Indeed, it wasn't until two years later (by which time I was qualified myself) that I observed – and successfully frustrated – another attempt at bumping off a new-born child.

But the episode of the obstetric house surgeon did reveal to me that even the most junior doctors were a little too prone to think that they could play God. I wasn't overkeen on doing this myself. (My experience has been that if you try and play God, you end up losing 3–1 in extra time.)

By the way, soon after that devastating conversation in the obstetrics department, it became clear just why limbless babies (and, indeed, earless babies) had begun appearing with alarming frequency on our maternity wards. It was quite simple. *All the mothers had been prescribed a 'harmless' tranquilliser*.

Its name was thalidomide.

*   *   *

Despite the pain and disappointment of delivering deformed babies, I loved my time in obstetric residence. The sheer fun of seeing this new, promising life born out of another one never palled for me – and never will.

Childbirth was admittedly a bit less romantic than I'd imagined; I could see why our superiors, the obstetricians of the 1960s, were notoriously reluctant to let husbands come in to see their wives deliver.

Said our senior registrar to us, 'Men like to think that women give birth on silk cushions, and they imagine that everything is beautiful and clean and nice. They just can't cope with the reality of blood and pain and shit.'

I've found it quite hard to write that last line; but unfortunately the fact is that childbirth is *indeed* a messy business – messy, but brave and wonderful. And, despite what we all believed in the 1960s about fathers being unable to 'cope' with blood, pain and excrement, the fact is that the last twenty-five years have shown that (mostly) they can.

Later that year, at another hospital, I was to find out that the presence of a father at the moment of birth could be a tremendous encouragement for the woman, and a genuine help in getting her through the delivery.

But first, I had one more experience to go through before

I finished my first spell of obstetric residency: conducting a birth *at home*.

*   *   *

For some reason, I decided to give the mother confidence by going to the delivery in my best suit and a brand new shirt.

The lifts were out of order in the tower block when I arrived together with the midwife – so we had to carry our bags up about six flights of stairs. This initial mechanical breakdown did not fill me with confidence! What if something went wrong with the delivery while the lifts were up the creek?

Still, the midwife was cheerful and very assured, and the mother-to-be's flat was warm and clean. Father was drifting around being useful, and Granny was busy making tea. The couple's previous child (a moppet of three or four) was peering in the bedroom door and demanding to know how soon the baby would arrive.

We reckoned it'd be about two or three hours, so the midwife pushed off down the long stairs again to go and see another case, leaving me in charge. Before she departed, she told me to spread newspapers thickly on the bed and all over the bedroom floor (a wise precaution) and to generally prepare everything for the delivery. I took off my jacket and got on with it.

I knew just what to say to the family, of course – because I'd heard the correct line of dialogue in about half a dozen movies.

'I shall want lots of hot water. . . .'

The hot water, in case you're interested, was jolly useful for sterilizing instruments and generally cleaning things up (including my hands). The family, a cheerful, co-operative lot, happily set about boiling up saucepans and helping me spread several dozen copies of the *Daily Express* (and probably the *Sporting Life*) all over the place. Pretty high-tech stuff, eh?

Fairly soon, I did another vaginal examination on the Mum – and found she was about to deliver a good deal sooner than we'd thought. I gulped. I was on my own, marooned by out-of-action lifts, about sixty feet up in the sky, in a flat with no telephone. *What if things went wrong?*

Thoughts of torrential bleeding and maternal collapse raced through my mind. And what about the baby? Oh God, what if it couldn't breathe?

If anything like *that* happened, no obstetric 'flying squad' (nor even a passing taxi driver or air hostess) was going to get here in time to help me out. Besides, they'd be absolutely knackered by running up the stairs.

Now if this were a novel or a TV play, we'd have sheer thrilling drama in this last bit: I'd find myself delivering unsuspected triplets with one hand, while doing a liver transplant on Father with the other.

In fact, nothing so sensational happened. The mother – a tough, sensible lady – did her very best to help me, and in next to no time I was delivering a bonny boy into her bed (and indeed, on to the *Daily Express*). At some stage in the proceedings, I vaguely heard a puffing midwife arrive behind me and say 'Oh good – all under control then. . . .'

Once I'd cut the cord, Granny swept up her new grandson in a shawl, and took him off to a cot. I remember that she was highly indignant because Dad unwisely suggested that she might have 'lost her touch' with babies.

So, it was all over bar the delivery of the placenta (that's the afterbirth). I remember kneeling by the big double bed and thinking how *capably* I had managed things.

Then . . . the mother suddenly fired out the placenta like a bullet blasting out of a gun. Pent up behind it was about a pint of blood and womb fluid, which *totally* saturated my brand new shirt.

Mum was perfectly OK after this experience. But before I could go back to the hospital, I had to sit around topless for an hour while Granny washed my shirt and drip-dried it out over the gas stove.

Very decent of her, I thought. Even more agreeable, the family did speculate enthusiastically about the idea of calling the baby David. But I think in the end they settled for Darren.

*   *   *

Well, that was the first spell of obstetric residency over. And before I started my second one, I spent a spot of useful time in our hospital's ante-natal clinic, helping to screen women at their regular check-ups in the months that led up to the birth of their babies.

I had the pleasure of learning how to 'turn' a baby that was the wrong way up – simply by pressing the mother's tummy with my hands. (Mind you, most of the sprogs promptly turned upside down again, just to spite me.)

Much of the screening work in the ante-natal clinics was routine and a bit boring. But I soon learned from the midwives that *it did save lives*. The simple routine of taking the lady's blood pressure, testing her urine for protein, and prodding her ankles (to see if they were boggy) is *invaluable* in helping to pick out women who are drifting into toxaemia of pregnancy – which is still one of the two most common killers of mothers.

Indeed, on the day I wrote this page, I sat on a General Medical Council committee which was judging the case of a GP who, for some reason, hadn't thought it worthwhile to do those three simple checks on an expectant Mum. As a result, she'd become desperately ill, and indeed lost her baby. In medicine, it's odd how often the application of a simple, dull routine (rather than, say, the prescription of a powerful drug) can save a life.

One feature of the ante-natal clinics has changed dramatically since those days: the pregnancy tests. It seems almost unbelievable now, but in the early 60s we had only recently dispensed with 'rabbit tests' for pregnancy – and were now relying on live *mouse and toad* tests to determine for certain whether a woman was expecting or not!

So rather a lot of unfortunate African toads (species *Xenopus laevis*) were kept in hospital labs, waiting to be injected with the urine of women who were thought to be pregnant.

They were then done in (the toads, not the women), and their ovaries were inspected to find out whether (say) HM the Queen or Jackie Kennedy or Christine Keeler was with child.

A few years later, cheap *chemical* tests for pregnancy came in, and the colonies of toads which had been kept hopping in hospital laboratories were quickly run down. It was the end of an era.

The mouse pregnancy test, by the way, was called the 'Ascheim-Zondek'. That was why (as I said earlier) it was claimed that at one London teaching hospital, the water in the nurses' swimming-pool was permanently 'Ascheim-Zondek positive'!

In contrast, detractors of the same hospital claimed that the water in the *medical students'* swimming-pool was likely to test positive for VD. . . .

*   *   *

I'm afraid that the sexual behaviour of medical students has indeed always tended to be slightly disreputable (a remarkable contrast with the dignified and worthy image of the medical profession itself). Perhaps this next bit will give you some idea of our sexual mores in the early 60s.

It was now time for me to push off from the medical school for a month, and get further experience of delivering babies – at a hospital located in a fashionable watering-place in the south of England.

The hospital's obstetric department was run by the legendary Lord Speculum – a man who had 'measured up' more rich and famous women than Christian Dior. His wards, I was glad to discover, were peaceful, gentle places. (This was nothing to do with him, incidentally – because he never went there. He was *far* too busy looking after the very, very rich.)

It was at that hospital where I first saw the joy of a real 'family confinement' – in other words, where the father took part and helped the mother through the last difficult hours. I remember in particular one big, fresh-faced country lady whose husband held her hand and kissed her and murmured in her ear as the pains grew stronger and more frequent. He was a simple sort of man, but he was a rock of support to her.

And when the baby was finally born and safely placed on the mother's breast, I saw the most extraordinary pink glow suffuse her face as she and her man looked down lovingly at what they'd created together. Not a moment one would easily forget.

There were plenty of babies being born in that spa town, so pretty soon I'd clocked up the total number of deliveries which are required of every would-be doctor.

My only other duty was to take an occasional turn at stitching up mothers who had 'torn', or who'd had episiotomy cuts. But episiotomies were fairly rare at that hospital, and because the midwives were very good indeed at their jobs, vaginal tears were relatively uncommon too. So I really didn't have to do very much vaginal embroidery.

Nevertheless, now that I was becoming moderately skilled at stitching, I did find it very satisfying to make a decent job of bringing the poor, torn tissues together, and suturing them neatly so that the woman would have the minimum of discomfort – and indeed, so that her subsequent sex life would (with luck) be happy and pain-free.

As one of my colleagues remarked to a mother who enquired why he was being so punctilious about repairing her nether regions, 'Ah well, m'dear: a thing of beauty is a joy forever. . . .'

And while we're on *that* particular subject, I may as well add that the sexual side of the hospital's social life was fairly remarkable.

The Permissive Society hadn't quite started yet – as you doubtless know, it actually began in the Beatle year of 1963, on about 24 May (at about half-past two in the afternoon, if memory serves me correctly).

But in that agreeable spa town, the effect of feeding a regular supply of extremely lusty London medical students into a community of sun-tanned, hormone-charged (and frequently frustrated) young pupil midwives was quite devastating. As a result, the Pre-Permissive Society had been going on there for years.

Astounding things took place in that institution: on one occasion while I was there, a night sister making her rounds disturbed a couple in gynaecology out-patients. The boy (a medical student, naturally) was of course *in flagrante delicto* between a pupil midwife's thighs – but those thighs were raised high up in the 'stirrups' which you find on the end of a couch in any gynaecology department. *Not* an easy situation to get out of quickly. . . .

Some well-meaning soul had put the medical students' residence right next to the midwives' home – which, of course, combined the maximum of temptation with the maximum of opportunity. As if this were not enough, we soon realised that at the nearby seaside, a philanthropist who was particularly well-disposed toward the hospital had placed a large and agreeable bathing chalet permanently at the disposal of the young midwives.

The sun shone most of that summer, and it was excellent swimming weather. So naturally, day after day the midwives took their boy-friends to the chalet for romantic dalliance. Some of them even managed to fit in a swim as well.

I understand that the chap who owned the next-door chalet was outraged at all this – particularly as his own bathing hut tended to be shaken rather violently from time to time by the vibrations from the adjoining building.

Certainly, on one memorable occasion during my stay, he turned almost purple with rage when he saw the same

medical student enter the chalet on three successive days –
with three successive midwives. (This is *not* the sort of
conduct that I would recommend to young gents or young
ladies in the Nervous Nineties – the risks are now far too
great.)

*   *   *

A romantic encounter of that summer of midwifery will
stay with me for the rest of my life.

Late one warm night, a group of medical students, young
midwives and off-duty doctors decided to drive out to a
secluded bay and have a bonfire on the beach. Inevitably,
the question of a midnight swim came up almost as soon as
we arrived. Equally inevitably, no one had any swimming gear. 'Let's all swim naked then!' cried the more
enthusiastic.

Well, plunging into the English Channel at midnight –
even in the middle of a hot summer – is a fairly marrow-
chilling experience. So I tore into the dark water at top
speed and struck out for almost fifty yards. Only then did I
lift my head out of the sea, tread water and look around.

Fairly predictably, a number of the others were still on
the beach, keeping warm by the bonfire; a few more were
frolicking nude or semi-nude in the shallows.

But out in the sea, a few yards in front of me, was one of
the loveliest women I'd ever seen. She must have had her
feet on a sandbank, because my first memory of her is that
the waves were washing gently around her beautiful
breasts, which she made no effort to conceal. Her white,
wet shoulders were magnificent, and her face was radiant.

Now you've probably read dozens of books in which
couples met in situations like this – and moments later were
wrapped in passionate sexual congress. But for us, it wasn't
like that at all.

All I remember is that I swam over to her and told her
how beautiful she was. Can you see a girl's blush in the
moonlight? I don't recall.

We talked for a few minutes, undisturbed by the revellers on the shore, then slowly waded in side by side and put on our clothes together. Then for a little while, we sat with our arms around each other by the fire before going chastely home.

For the rest of my stay in that pleasant sun-drenched town I saw her every day. Whenever she was off duty from the midwifery department, we would rush to meet each other, and then set off on foot or on bicycles to explore the quiet country lanes outside the town. I remember how at night we strolled through the velvet darkness of the cliff walks, watching glow-worms magically lighting up the bushes. On rainy days, we'd cycle far out on to the moors, then shelter from the weather under some abandoned railway arch, exchanging long, long kisses.

Her kisses had a curious creamy quality that I'd encountered in no other woman. Because she spent so many of her working hours in dishing out feeds to babies, we used to classify those kisses of hers as if they were types of milk: 'skimmed', 'semi-skimmed', 'half-cream', and – best of all – 'full cream'.

You'll doubtless assume that it must have gone a great deal further than a romantic exchange of full-cream kisses. But the fact was that though she let me enjoy the glory of the magnificent breasts which I'd first seen in the moonlit sea, we never had intercourse, and I never tried to persuade her into it.

Why not? Because, most unusually for an English girl in those days, she had become engaged to a businessman living in Eastern Europe. She hadn't seen him for six months and was clearly pretty ambivalent in her feelings towards him. But she wore his ring on her finger, and that was enough. Though for a while my mind was filled with dreams of her and her kisses, I knew that there could be no future for us, and so did she.

We did spend the night together twice before I went back to London. But on each occasion, she slept in my bed while

I slept alongside her on the floor, holding her hand throughout the night.

So ended my romance with the lovely, sun-kissed midwife. But every summer for the next few years, I made a point of sending off a dozen tins of Cornish cream to an address in faraway Eastern Europe. . . .

I expect they all got pinched by the border guards.

*   *   *

I forgot to tell you about Lord Speculum, who (you'll recall) was the obstetric 'king' of the spa town. This man had one of the most amazing private practices in the country – a practice which brought him vast sums of money from titled and rich ladies.

The number of private deliveries he did each year was prodigious, and it was hard to see how he could fit them all in. There were days when he seemed to be delivering Lady —— at one end of the country while simultaneously doing a private hysterectomy on the Honourable Mrs —— in a nursing home fifty miles away.

From time to time, he told people that he was going to cut down on his private practice – by doubling his fees. All that happened was that his practice became even *more* popular: women simply loved being delivered by an obstetrician who was so very, very expensive!

Late one night I was having a cup of coffee with the sister who helped him with most of his private deliveries. I asked her how on earth he managed to find time to conduct all these private births.

'Oh, it's quite simple,' she said airily. 'He doesn't.'

'He doesn't?'

'That's right. A lot of the time, he doesn't get to the delivery at all. But we always give the mother plenty of gas – and tell her afterwards that he popped in at the last minute and delivered the baby.'

I sat absolutely astounded at this revelation – but it didn't strike Sister as at all odd that Lord Speculum was taking large sums of money from these women under false pretences.

She went on to explain that it didn't really matter if Lord S was hundreds of miles away operating on somebody else when a 'private' baby was born: the parents were always told that *he* had delivered it. And the Mum was so full of drugs that she couldn't tell the difference.

Sister added, 'We even had a baby born in the bed once.' She meant that it arrived between the sheets before anyone had realised that the mother was just about to give birth.

'And we STILL managed to convince the woman that his lordship had popped in and delivered it. We just told her that she must have been a bit delirious!'

So that was the foundation of Lord Speculum's famous private practice, the envy of many a medical man. Soon afterwards he retired, very rich indeed.

In the years before his death, he became really quite well known in the media – as a commentator on medical ethics.

11

ALL WORK AND NO PLAY . . .

A MEDICAL STUDENT who had made himself thoroughly objectionable to his colleagues discovered late one night that their wrath could be terrible indeed. They seized him, took him to the room where plaster of Paris was stored, and applied that remarkably quick-drying material to his arms, legs and body.

Next morning, he was found immobile and furious, propped up against the wall near the front door. All of him was encased in the rigid white plaster, except his face. And his genitals.

*   *   *

Now this very cruel jape may not strike you as fitting in too well with the image of a caring, sensitive profession. And I'm afraid I have to admit that the off-duty behaviour of medical students is frequently quite appalling.

But I think that by now you can see *why*, throughout the ages, they've by tradition behaved foolishly or outrageously or promiscuously or drunkenly in their (very limited) spare time – simply as a sort of antidote to the stresses and tragedies of their working lives.

Anyway, what I'm going to do in this chapter is to tell you a bit about the frequently over-the-top way in which we spent our off-duty hours – but also I'm going to try and provide a counterpoint made up of some of the sad and traumatic experiences which (I believe) made us behave more than a little crazily at times.

*   *   *

At a male-only party in the students' residence (which, I'm rather glad to say, I did *not* attend), twenty or thirty future doctors decided that in order to investigate the physiology of the kidney, they would keep drinking beer all night until they had filled the entire bath with urine. Charming!

When I chatted to a couple of the survivors in the morning, they *thought* they'd succeeded. But they weren't very sure, because one of them had for some reason spent part of the night hanging on a rope outside the bathroom window, while the other one occasionally tried to rescue him.

Unfortunately, the cult of excessive booze – which has harmed so many medical men – was already taking hold. A psychiatrist who I worked with said to me once, 'When I look back on my medical student career, I see the case history of a psychopath – and an alcoholic psychopath at that.'

Not far off, squire – not far off.

*   *   *

'You'd better have a look at the man without a face in the long-stay ward,' said one of the doctors to me.

I duly made my way to the ward, where a male nurse took me to the patient's bedside, started unravelling the bandages which covered his entire head (except for a small hole over the mouth area), and gave me a brief history of the case.

Apparently, many years ago the man – now aged about fifty – had developed a small sore patch on his left cheek. It was, in fact, a rodent ulcer: an extremely common form of skin cancer which is very easily cured if caught early enough. Unfortunately, nothing had been done about this particular rodent ulcer, partly because the man was simple-minded and had scarcely noticed it himself. There must have come a moment when a doctor looked at it and realised what it was – but by then, it would have been too late.

As the nurse took off the last of the bandages, I could see why the ulcer was called 'rodent'. Like a rat, it had eaten away three-quarters of his face. The patient's left cheek, his left eye and his nose had all gone – and had been replaced by a hideous pink-rimmed crater, lined with a thin film of yellowy-green pus. I think there was a sightless remnant of a right eye somewhere just inside the edge of the ever-expanding crater. The mouth would soon be engulfed, and then perhaps this tragic life would be over.

The man said nothing; in fact, I am doubtful if he was still capable of speech, poor soul. The nurse replaced the sticky bandages – and I went home for my tea.

* * *

When we went berserk and drank too much and got up to silly pranks, the consultants were remarkably tolerant – presumably because they themselves had once been through such a phase too.

For instance, the sub-dean (a grizzled, much-respected surgeon) was revered by us – not just for his very considerable surgical skills, but because in his medical student days he had one night driven a Baby Austin car in through the doors of the Casualty department.

Turning right, he had carried on down the quarter-mile of hospital corridors till he reached the massive lifts. Without hesitation, he drove the little car into a lift, took it up to the first floor, and then accelerated away along further corridors till he reached the double doors of the theatre suite. Having negotiated these, he proceeded to park the Austin neatly in the centre of the deserted operating theatre, right next to the table.

It was found there next morning, and allegedly no one objected very much except for Sister – who was reputed to have said, 'How many times do I have to tell the students not to bring unsterile objects into my theatre?'

*   *   *

While I was examining one of the aforementioned surgeon's patients, I asked her to remove her brassière – and found what was virtually an inoperable tumour underneath it.

The woman was a pleasant lady of fifty-five or so. She had noticed a lump in her breast perhaps a year ago, but had hoped it would go away (as women so often do). It didn't.

Indeed, the tumour had already grown savagely outwards, and had fastened itself into her skin, so that touching her breast was like putting your fingertips on a large chunk of discoloured, bumpy rock. And the huge, craggy glands which I could feel in her armpit indicated that the cancer had already spread extensively. Radiotherapy would shrink the tumour but would not save her life.

Once again, I felt furious at the fact that people just didn't *know* the early signs of cancer; or if they did, they often hid the cancer away, hoping that it would disperse on its own. Time and again, lives were being wasted – lives like hers.

Like many of the patients, she sought to find a simple explanation for her problem.

'I work in a fish-and-chip shop, doctor,' she said. 'And I'm always reaching up with this arm to get things off the top shelf. I think it's all that stretching that's caused it, don't you?'

God knows whether I agreed or not – I don't recall. What I *am* sure of is that nobody told her she had cancer. She, like all the others in her plight, was just allowed to think that she had 'a little problem in the breast that needed some ray treatment.'

For in the 1960s, the doctrine which was taught to us was this:

Don't tell patients that they have cancer;

Don't tell them they're going to die.

I disagreed considerably with these rules, but no one was very interested in a student's viewpoint. There were admittedly exceptions to the rules but, at that time, consultants tended to brush aside most patients' queries about their illnesses with remarks like, 'You've got an ulcer in the bowel, Mr Fortescue – and we'll take it away for you on Monday morning. Good-day.'

Astonishingly, views have greatly changed these days, and there now seems to be a lot more honesty about telling patients what their chances are. But the doctors who taught us were quite firm that you did *not* tell the patient he had cancer (though you usually deputed one of your junior doctors – totally untrained in communication, of course – to pass the news on to his wife).

However, in fairness, I must stress that our consultants behaved like this out of kindness – an arrogant kindness maybe, but they *were* doing what they thought was best. And as I say, they did make exceptions. . . .

One of our senior surgeons decided to tell a private patient (p'raps it's significant that he was private) the bad news that he had an inoperable cancer of the prostate, and could not expect to live much longer than a year.

He did this on the basis of his clinical examination alone, without carrying out the confirmatory test called a 'biopsy' – in which a small piece of tissue is removed for examination under the microscope.

The patient was a very rich man, and when Mr X told him that he only had about twelve months to live, and had better put his affairs in order, he took the advice as gospel.

He disposed of large amounts of his investments, donated huge sums to charity, dished out cash to various relatives, and then set out on an agreeable money-no-object final tour of the world.

A year later, he was still feeling perfectly well (if a good deal poorer) and decided it might be time to seek a second opinion.

The second opinion was quite clear, as were the third and fourth opinions. He did not have cancer at all; he might well live to a very ripe old age. So he sued the surgeon.

Mr X was ready to defend the case, on the basis that he had *not* been negligent, but had simply been deceived by the unusual feel of the patient's prostate. In court, he contended that a man of his experience did not *need* to do a confirmatory biopsy in order to make his diagnosis.

Opposing counsel rose to cross-examine, and produced a large surgical textbook in evidence.

'Is this a standard textbook, Mr X?'

'It is.'

'Will you read us the sentence I have marked in the chapter on cancer of the prostate?'

'Yes. It says: "A biopsy must be done in *every* case. Under no circumstances must the surgeon rely on clinical examination alone. . . ."'

'And now will you tell us who is the author of that chapter, Mr X?'

'Yes. I am.'

Disaster for Mr X – and proof to the students that the consultants were not as infallible as they seemed. Yet, curiously, the sympathy in the hospital for years afterwards was with Mr X – partly because his career had more or less been ruined by the case.

'Just like those bloody lawyers,' said one doctor who I asked about the affair. 'Fancy using old X's textbook as a stick to beat him with!'

Medical loyalty, you see, is very strong – and perhaps understandably so. When a doctor has his career torn apart in the courts, it's very hard not to think 'There but for the grace of God . . .'

*   *   *

The behaviour of the hospital's rugby club was perhaps the best demonstration of my theory that medical students, working under considerable stress, desperately need to let off steam.

Their boozing and wenching (at least, *attempted* wenching – it's very difficult to wench successfully when you've been boozing) were legendary. On the field, they were often immensely courageous. But since they were usually pitched against older, bigger opponents who actually had time to *train*, they lost and lost and lost.

I played for the hospital first and second XV's throughout most of my medical career (which is probably one reason why they kept losing), and I remember that at one time I hadn't been on a winning side for *three years*!

We lost to better, heftier, fitter teams by prodigious scores; we lost to remarkably poor sides because several of our players didn't turn up till half-time (having lunched over-well in the pub): we went to rugby festivals and lost because our team were so hungover from the debaucheries of the night before that they could hardly find their way on to the pitch. Oh dear, oh dear, oh dear. . . .

Like many rugby clubs, we had a most unfortunate and silly habit of trying to acquire 'souvenirs' while away from home. On one occasion, the first XV went on tour to France and decided to prise a French doctor's expensive marble nameplate off the wall outside his consulting room. (They would not have considered this as stealing, you understand.)

With commendable restraint, the French police simply impounded their passports – and waited grimly until the rapidly-sobering medical students pooled all their remaining funds and handed over enough money to buy the doctor a new nameplate.

Our experiences with the British police were slightly less lucky. On one occasion, the hospital first XV were due to play Metropolitan Police E-Division (I understand that they are the gents who patrol much of the West End of London).

With our usual shambolic approach, we turned up late for the game. By the time we'd got ourselves together in the dressing-room, the police XV had been waiting on the pitch for ten or fifteen minutes. We totally failed to realise that this had made them *very* irritated indeed.

When the referee started the match, they sailed into us with fists, heads and boots. I had never seen anything like it in my life. Within minutes, several medical students were lying stunned and bleeding in various corners of the pitch.

However, one thing you could say about our dotty and ill-organised team was this: we were *not* dirty players.

To our credit, we made no significant retaliation throughout a vile game in which the police team – watched by a senior officer – committed a long series of brutal assaults on us. The referee was unable to control the coppers, nor could their captain (who seemed a reasonable enough bloke) do much. The only satisfaction was that they were so busy hitting and gouging and kicking that, for once, we actually won the match.

But just before the end of the game, a fist exploded on my right eye (in which I had a large, old-fashioned, hard plastic contact lens). A frightening dark patch suddenly developed across my field of vision, and I was carted off to Casualty.

For a week I was treated as a potential case of detached retina – which means, of course, that my sight was in danger – but I'm glad to say that the dark shadow eventually receded and my eyesight returned to normal.

I'd better add that I found it very hard to cope with the events of that day. Like most middle-class British children I'd grown up believing that 'our policemen were wonderful.' Now, here were men who would viciously kick and head-butt silly but innocent medical students – simply because we had kept them waiting.

Fortunately, soon afterwards I had proof that not all policemen were like that. We were due to meet another Metropolitan Police side, and were fairly terrified at the prospect – especially as we'd been told that the police teams were no longer allowed to play each other, because of the carnage that ensued!

But when we got to Hendon Police College sports grounds, we found our opponents amiable as lambs. We had a lovely, fair match with them – only marred by the fact that we couldn't get a drink for an hour afterwards because of the licensing laws.

'Sorry not to bend the rules,' said their captain. 'But there's too many bloody coppers round here.'

*   *   *

Back at the medical school, we spent long hours in the pathology museum, where the most flesh-creeping monstrosities were kept in glass jars along the shelves. It was like a library of horrors.

Babies with two heads; babies with an eye in the centre of the forehead; twin babies hopelessly sharing one set of legs – all had been born to some poor woman, and had promptly been pickled and put in jars for our education.

In fact, the pathology museum was a most useful place for learning, and I spent an enormous amount of time there with my brilliant friend Mike, working our way through transparent pots that contained practically every cancer that afflicts man – a lump of someone's cancerous liver or brain here, a bit of somebody's cancerous penis or testicle there. Most of them (according to the typed reference folder which gave details of every specimen) were monuments to human tragedy, though in a few cases the patient had survived, even though part of him (infected or cancerous or bullet-riddled) had ended up embalmed in a pickling jar in our museum.

Not altogether surprisingly, when I had a spinal disc taken out of my back some years ago, I promptly had it put in a glass pot, and it now stands in my study.

*   *   *

The hospital rugby club's annual dinner was like a sexual megalomaniacs' night out. Looking back, I shudder at the thought of fifty future doctors and dentists pouring gallons of beer into themselves as fast as possible, throwing bangers and mash around the room, and bellowing out drunken songs and stories that involved every sexual and scatological perversion known to man and goat.

(I hope that our successors of today are slightly more sensible – but I understand that their annual dinner does still include a trifle-flinging contest. . . .)

Surprisingly, these dreadful revels were as a rule presided over by one of the more venerable hospital consultants (the president of the rugby club), who did at least bring a slight trace of sophistication to the proceedings by telling jokes that did not consist merely of a string of four-letter words.

I can still see him – all respectability in his magnificent Harley Street double-breasted suit – rising to his feet, quelling the alcoholic hubbub around him with an authoritative gesture, and launching into a story about two 'chaps' who were on a country railway platform one Monday morning.

'So the first chap got into the train, and he leaned out of the carriage window and he said to the second chap: "My dear fellow – thank you for a simply marvellous weekend. And I must tell you: your wife is the best fuck in the County."'

We shivered in delicious horror, almost unable to believe that such a word could have fallen from a consultant's august lips. . . .

'So the train started, and another chap who was sitting in the carriage said, "Excuse me, old boy, but I couldn't help overhearing what you said about Blenkinsop's wife. *Surely* it's not true?"

'"Er . . . well it's *not*, actually."

'"Good heavens! Then why on earth did you say it?"

'"Well, you see; it's just that he's *such* an awfully decent fellow."'

Mr Woffington-Smythe sat down to a storm of applause from those of us who were still sober enough to understand the joke (which was not many).

You may be surprised that hospital consultants supported the rugby club even in such boozy and dotty excesses. But the fact is that in Britain (and Ireland), rugby – with its social cachet – has always been 'the doctors' game'. Even at the time when I'm writing, there are two or three qualified doctors – and a dentist – among the four British Isles international fifteens.

Somehow the consultants seemed to approve of the 'chaps' playing rugby – as they themselves had done thirty or forty years before. At medical school admission interviews, would-be students were frequently asked if they were useful scrum-halves or could kick goals (and that was only the girls!). And there was a general feeling that chaps who'd done well for the hospital XV might perhaps be favoured for those desperately sought-after house surgeon jobs after they'd qualified.

A lot of this wildly irrational pro-rugby attitude seemed to stem from what was (and is) far and away the most sport-orientated of all Britain's medical schools: St Mary's Hospital, London.

St Mary's was so obsessed with rugby (and so successful at it) that it was rumoured among us that the dean of the medical school used to go down to the docks to meet the boat from South Africa, where he'd approach any broad-shouldered lads and say ''Scuse me: d'you fancy a career in medicine by any chance?'

This daft story did have a certain tenuous origin in fact. For the truth was that many years before, St Mary's had been in a terrible state. Its academic reputation was so poor that very few young people wanted to go there to study medicine. The dean of those days was Lord Moran (later Churchill's personal doctor), and he came up with a brilliant – if eccentric – scheme to revitalise the place.

He reasoned that if St Mary's could win the Hospitals' Cup Rugby competition (and *keep* winning it) then the resultant publicity would attract large numbers of would-be doctors to come and study at St Mary's. So, he rapidly began to recruit rugby internationals (Welsh, South African, whatever) as medical students – with the inevitable result that St Mary's soon won the Cup. Before very long, the image of his hospital had soared sky-high – and medical students were flocking to get in!

So, incredibly, Lord Moran had been proved right – even though the rest of the London hospitals laughed at his efforts and liked to pretend that St Mary's men were OK at sport, but not too clear about the dose of aspirin.

Ever since then, Moran's Medical School has continued the same extraordinary policy of picking outstanding sportsmen and trying to make them into doctors. Some of these blokes turned out very well – for instance, the world's first four-minute miler, Roger Bannister, who is now an excellent neurologist.

But it does seem a slightly odd way of picking medical students, doesn't it? At other medical schools the same thing goes on in a more minor way: for example, a few years back my own hospital rather amazingly gave a place to the new Miss World immediately after she'd won the competition! (Admittedly, she'd already done some medical studies in India.)

I believe that she qualified successfully; but the same isn't true of some of the poor lads who were given medical school places simply because they were outstanding rugby players.

Most hospitals had at least one chap who'd been admitted to the medical school on the sole ground that he was built like a gorilla and had already played rugger for his county or country. Lots of these guys lingered on at their hospitals for years and years, failing exam after exam but being given endless reprieves from expulsion. After about half a decade of this, they were usually encouraged to take up dentistry instead of medicine; this was regarded as less intellectually demanding, but still allowed them to play for the hospital XV! Another six or seven years of failing dental exams might follow before they were gently pitched out of the hospital in their early thirties.

One of our beery rugby stalwarts followed this sad pattern but, to his great credit, did eventually succeed in qualifying as a dentist after some *thirteen years* as a student.

*   *   *

Meanwhile, back on the wards my mates and I were busy examining Mr Cornwell – a charming, dapper, middle-aged man who was the very height of suburban respectability: a thoroughly nice chap whose life was unfortunately being made a misery by violent shooting pains round his ribs, and also by the fact that he could no longer walk properly.

His symptoms made no great sense to me, but he himself had no doubt of the diagnosis; he'd seen a number of doctors over the last few years, and they'd told him what was wrong. . . .

'It's the stress of the war that did it to me, boys,' he announced. 'And I'm very lucky really, because lots of fellows came out of the war with far worse than me. So I've got a lot to be thankful for, haven't I?'

Poor nice Mr Cornwell: doubtless he *had* been through enormous stress and strain during World War II – but no amount of stress gives you constant vicious pain and makes you walk like a dislocated camel.

In fact, the illness which he attributed to 'the stress of the war' was actually tertiary syphilis.

Doubtless an encounter twenty years before with some dark-eyed girl in Italy or France had left him this terrible legacy. The penicillin jabs which our houseman gave him stopped the disease from progressing any further – so that at least he wouldn't go barking mad (like so many syphilis victims before him). But for the rest of his life, he would lurch into his masonic lodge meetings and his local charity functions with the spavined gait of someone whose nervous system is shot to pieces. And he would be racked by the terrible 'lightning pains' which indicated that the germ had hacked its brutal way through great chunks of his spinal cord.

So sex had done this to him. I shuddered at the thought that the activity which was so infinitely agreeable to most of us could have such painful and tragic consequences.

*   *   *

Somewhere about this stage of our careers, we decided to build a bomb.

This was an act of unbelievable stupidity. Seeing that we knew just how easily the human body could be ripped apart by accidents and violence, I find it hard now to understand how we got involved in anything so silly. But we did.

There was at least no malice at all in our action, and our bomb was not intended to hurt anyone. The situation was this.

The students' cramped little house of residence (which had seen so many debauched parties and indecent matings) was about to be demolished by the hospital authorities in order to make way for something bigger and grander. We decided to save them the trouble – by simply blowing it up in one final, grand, Wagnerian, celebratory conflagration.

Since we were scientists (well, sort of) we knew how to make an explosive device. Incredibly, or so it seems almost thirty years later, we went down to the local chemist's shop and bought all the materials from him, telling him – in a very curious version of the truth – that we were 'doing some tricky research into the nitrate ion. . . .'

It never occurred to us that if we'd been caught, the pharmacist would get into trouble too. And, arrogant as we were, it also never occurred to us that our home-made bomb might go off prematurely and kill or maim somebody (us, for instance).

Well, by the time we'd finished making our device it was spherical, about two foot across, painted black, and with a long fuse sticking out of the top. Perhaps we should have gone all the way and printed 'BOMB' on it.

Late one night we crept into the abandoned house, planted the massive black orb in the basement, lit the fuse and fled.

Thirty seconds later, there was a colossal bang and the house shuddered. A sheet of flame shot through the basement and then, much to our surprise, subsided. Our ludicrous bomb had achieved no more than to startle the mice – and slightly singe the basement stairs.

Shortly thereafter, I was on duty in Casualty during Guy Fawkes' night. With the pomposity so typical of many a young medical man, I spent a good deal of the evening loftily telling burned and singed people that they really ought to be *much* more careful with fireworks in future. . . .

*   *   *

Somewhere in the midst of all this, we were told to examine a man who had something wrong with his penis.

When we peeled back the sheets – the phrase 'something wrong' seemed to be a bit of an understatement. Most of his organ had simply disappeared and had been replaced by a huge, red angry-looking swelling.

'What's that?' said one of the lads in bewilderment.

'It's a granuloma, of course,' said the Firm Swot witheringly. (He had, of course, looked up the diagnosis in the patient's notes.)

A passing registrar discreetly explained to us that a granuloma is a chronic and destructive inflammatory swelling – rare (thank heavens). There was no hope for the poor bloke's penis – about two-thirds of which would have to be amputated, leaving him with only a tiny stump.

Soon afterwards, the consultant urologist arrived to

conduct his ward round. Throwing back the sheets, he examined the dejected man's organ, in full view of the rest of the ward.

'What's happened to this, then?' he asked the patient. 'Mice been at it?'

I expect he thought that this was a good way of cheering the poor guy up.

*   *   *

Every year, the students of the twelve London Teaching Hospitals competed in an overnight walk from London to Brighton, many of them dressed as surgeons or nurses, and carrying stethoscopes or bedpans. (The *real* nurses would set up first-aid tents on the grass verges all the way down the Brighton road to care for the footsore and the collapsed.) I don't know what the motorists hammering up the A23 thought of this fantastically attired medical army coming at them through the night, but it must have been a nasty shock.

As the captain of the hospital athletics team, I thought it my duty to *run* all the way to Brighton, oblivious of the fact that the distance was fifty-six miles, and I had done no training.

The start of the race was at the Tower of London at 6 p.m. Precisely on time, a purple-faced major-general rose above the crowd of several hundred weirdly-attired medics and fired a gun. We were off.

Wearing a placard calling for 'MORE PAY FOR NURSES', I crossed Tower Bridge and jogged my way through South London, Croydon, Purley and Redhill. Way behind me were medics who'd decided to drink in every pub on the way (at least till closing time); medics dressed as lions; medics dressed as gorillas; even four medics in operating gear, pushing a theatre trolley on which reposed a 'patient' on the receiving end of a Guinness drip.

(Messrs. Guinness sponsored the race. Very shrewdly, they had always been strong supporters of the medical profession and of medical students. Some years before they'd sent a crate of Guinness to every doctor in the country – and had then used the thank-you letters in their adverts: 'Wonderful stuff, your Guinness – signed L.R.C.P., M.R.C.S., Swansea.')

Some miles south of Gatwick Airport, my legs gave out and I subsided indignantly into the first-aid tent run by the nurses of St Thomas's Hospital. Several hours later, totally disabled by blisters, I was mortified to be passed by the Guinness drip party – who eventually got through to Brighton the following afternoon in a finishing time of about seventeen hours or so.

Much more embarrassing than my blistered collapse was the most spectacular casualty of the race. In the middle of the night, a medical student decided to break off for ten minutes and take his girl-friend into the Surrey woods for a swift spot of love-play. Like many young men before him, he managed to rip her vagina with a jagged fingernail and cause a fairly torrential haemorrhage. He made various frantic attempts to staunch the flow with borrowed sanitary towels, but the poor lass eventually had to be taken off in an ambulance to Crawley General Hospital.

Somehow, the episode seemed to embody just what the average medical student knew about sexual technique. . . .

The crazy Inter-Hospitals Brighton Walk continued for several more years in the 1960s – until the inevitable occurred, and a girl medic was killed by a car. The age of the automobile had finally made the A23 far too dangerous for even us dotty lot to walk or run beside it.

*   *   *

The forensic medicine department's annual lecture presentation called 'Abortion, Infanticide and Rape' was the most popular one on the course. The lecture theatre, in which the more boring consultants sometimes addressed an audience of only three, four or five students, was packed out with well over a hundred people.

Why? Heaven knows, since abortion, infanticide and rape are all pretty revolting subjects. Perhaps it was the fact that this lecture, along with the one on the 'Dutch Cap', comprised the only teaching on sex in the whole five years.

The section on abortion was absolutely *awful* – but, alas, very necessary, in view of the fact that the horrors of back-street terminations were so common in those days (shortly before safe, legalised abortion came in). We were presented with ghastly slides of dead girls lying on beds, with rubber syringes coming out of their vaginas; slides of tiny babies curled up in lavatory pans; glass jars containing lethally infected wombs – infected by somebody's blundering attempts at illegal abortion; and, finally, examples of knitting needles and crochet hooks with which desperate women had tried to terminate themselves – usually with disastrous results.

The fact that several of the boys had paid for back-street abortions for their girl-friends added a certain sad piquancy to the occasion.

The section on infanticide was equally appalling. Infanticide is the crime of killing a child under a year old, by its mother. (English law – in a curious burst of humaneness – has long recognised that women who are newly delivered of children are often in a rather disordered emotional state; therefore the law adjudges that a female who kills her own infant is guilty of a lesser crime than murder; namely, infanticide.)

As you can imagine, this section of the presentation was equally gruesome: specimens of strangled babies, suffocated babies, babies who had been picked up by the heels so that their heads could be smashed against the sink. . . .

The only good thing about the lectures from my point of view was that I found I could face it all with relative equanimity. Back at school five years previously, when I'd looked at pictures of such things in a forensic medicine textbook, I'd virtually been sick.

The final section of the presentation was about rape. As

you probably know, many people think that rape is an agreeably salacious subject: hence its popularity in the saucier Sunday newspapers (and hence the high attendance at this particular lecture). In fact, rape is the most hideous and degrading business.

Nowadays, I know this for certain – having examined and tried to counsel a good few women whose entire lives have been ruined by the gross brutality which they suffered during a rape.

I hope I knew it that morning in the lecture theatre, as we waded through pictures of girls with their breasts badly bitten and their thighs torn by fingernails; pictures of girls beaten up or murdered; and examples of evidence, in the shape of ripped underwear and semen-stained trouser-buttons.

However, the lasting impression which the forensic medicine consultant (a witty and articulate old cove) gave us was not exactly a caring one; it was this: *be very cynical indeed about women's accusations of rape*. He told us with utter assurance that:

(a) many girls give in to a chap – and then decide three weeks later that it was rape;

(b) many other girls make up fantastic accusations about rape when nobody's so much as laid a finger on them.

Well, of course, I now know that there was just a grain of truth in what he taught us. For instance, I remember a case in which a young woman visited her GP to ask him to confirm that she was pregnant. She then went to the police and announced that the doctor was the father of her baby – and that it had been rape.

The doctor protested his innocence, but was taken down to the station and put in a cell. Some hours later, the poor girl confessed: the real father of the baby was her *brother* – and she'd falsely accused the GP because she had been desperate to find a 'respectable' Dad for the baby.

Despite such occasional bizarre happenings, the fact remains that the incidence of rape and sexual interference is disturbingly high (a fact which my own recent national sex surveys have confirmed). And it's far greater than most doctors realised in those rather smug days of the 1960s.

Yet the message which our consultant drummed into us that morning was this: the police *know* whether a woman has been raped or not – so believe them if they say she's lying! A hundred or so young students walked out of the lecture theatre with that extraordinarily crass and irrational thought drummed into their ears. Some of them doubtless kept it with them for the rest of their lives – though I hope that many eventually had the sense to see how silly it was.

A year or so later, I somehow won the hospital's forensic medicine prize, in an exam set by the above-mentioned consultant. I was profoundly lucky that there were no questions on rape.

*   *   *

So there we are. I hope that you can see that as our final year approached, we'd been through some fairly shattering and challenging experiences – experiences of a sort which the average person quite simply *never* has to face.

It's not altogether surprising therefore that so many of us reacted by behaving in wild, drunken or promiscuous ways when we were at play. After all, 'play' was soon to come to an end as our qualifying exams drew near. . . .

Have medical students changed and become sober and sensible? I don't think so. The final of the Inter-Hospitals Rugby Cup is still an occasion for mass mayhem on the scale of the Battle of Waterloo (with flour, soot and water replacing the gunfire).

And not too long ago, my attention was drawn to the case of a medical student who was up in court because, in a state of mild inebriation, he had gallantly intervened in a fight and attempted to disable the man who he judged to be the aggressor. The method he used had at least the merit of being anatomically well-informed: he squeezed the gentleman's testicles. Alas, the gent in question turned out to be a police officer.

Letting the medical student off with a caution, the magistrate advised him, 'You must not take the Law into your own hands.'

12

THE LAST YEAR

I WAS NOW twenty-two, and my medical school career (after its very shaky start) was going well – especially as I no longer feared seeing people with their heads or legs hanging off. But now there was a new fear on the horizon: our qualifying exams, which would (we desperately hoped) make us into doctors.

The last year of a medical student's training, leading up to those exams, is particularly tough: there are so many new subjects to cram into it, plus the massive effort of revising so much of what you've tried to learn over the past five years.

Faced with this vast amount of work during my final twelve months, I rather bizarrely decided to continue running the hospital athletics club and also to go on playing rugby whenever I could. It wasn't a bad decision really, because it helped to keep me sane, by taking my mind off work for a few hours each week.

I made one other reasonably sensible choice during the course of that last frenetic year: because I was in a state of considerable emotional turmoil over the end of an unhappy love affair, I opted to more or less give up sex (apart from the purely therapeutic DIY kind) for a while. To spend a period of time without chasing girls did at least remove one complication from my life for some months! It also gave me

175

more chance to study the hundred or so medical textbooks which I'd bought over the past few years.

Alas, several of my friends *didn't* choose to spend their final year in relative chastity, and so they had the usual complexities of love to cope with as they struggled desperately to revise.

Alan – who, like several of my friends, was Catholic Irish – was traumatically ditched by his fiancée during his last year. He promptly took up with an older, more experienced woman, who astounded him by introducing him to oral sex.

To his chagrin, he found that while he enjoyed this activity enormously, he was totally overwhelmed by guilt about fellatio and cunnilingus. And for some reason he was utterly disgusted by the sight of this poor woman writhing about on the floor in the throes of a tongue-induced climax: all this ecstasy was something he just couldn't cope with.

So, ditching her, he moved on and spent most of his final year going with prostitutes: a pastime as expensive as it was dangerous. It was especially risky for him because, like one or two others in our year, he firmly believed that it was a sin to wear a condom.

He'd been indoctrinated in this attitude by his 'father figure' – a nice elderly priest who regularly heard his confession. When poor old Alan admitted he'd been with a woman yet again, Father O'Rhythm was ever tolerant and understanding. But he always asked, 'And did you wear a French letter, me son?'

If Alan replied 'No', the Father inevitably said, 'Ah well, that's no so bad then. . . .'

Alan and I argued endlessly about this point during our last year. He couldn't see that using a sheath must surely make a sexual sin *lesser*, rather than greater. After all, the Father had told him that if one decided to approve of intercourse with sheaths, one therefore 'removed the only possible objection to homosexuality.'

Surprised? Well, the basis of Father O'Rhythm's

remarkable doctrine was that if it were morally OK to achieve a climax through contact between your penis and a rubber sheath, then it would have to be equally OK in moral terms to achieve your climax up another gentleman's bottom! And since homosexuality was *clearly* wicked, then condoms must also be wicked. . . .

I was never able to convince Alan of the fairly obvious logical flaw in this argument. So, he staggered through his final year, regularly having fear-ridden and completely unprotected sex with ladies of doubtful virtue and even more doubtful health. Not altogether surprisingly, he soon became quite ill and was unable to sit his exams (though he did, I'm glad to say, qualify some time later).

*   *   *

This may be the moment to describe what all these fornicating medical students (and I'm afraid that about eighty per cent of them *were* fornicating) were using for contraception in that last twelve months or so before they became doctors.

A proportion, maybe a quarter, were using the condom (usually bought in a disguised voice and with *great* embarrassment from the herbalist/truss supplier just down the road from the hospital).

Nearly everybody else was relying on a rather lunatic combination of withdrawal and the safe period.

Withdrawal, aka *coitus interruptus* (or, as one of my patients once called it, 'the old *cautious interruptus*, doc') was extremely widespread in all classes of society at that time – and indeed, about five per cent of couples still blunder along with it today.

Just in case you don't know what it means, the idea is that at the crucial moment, the gent 'pulls out' and comes all over the lady's tummy or thigh. *Not* exactly very romantic or satisfying – and, as you can imagine, it led to a great deal of frustration (not to mention a great deal of anxiety about pregnancy) among the nursing profession.

The rhythm method (also known as the 'safe period') was the other great medical student standby of the 1960s. From various surreptitious sources, most of us had gleaned the fact that you were *reasonably* safe if you didn't make love to a girl between the tenth and eighteenth days of her cycle.

But there was lots of confusion about this. (It was alleged that when an Irish student was asked during his finals to 'define the safe period', he replied: 'Half-time in the match against Wales, sor!')

One book which I consulted had the safe period dates completely the wrong way round – which meant that if you'd followed its dotty advice, you'd have made love only during the *fertile* times of the girl's month.

So, your average medic stumbled on through the sexual encounters of that final year – 'pulling out' when he thought his girl-friend was fertile, but climaxing inside her when he thought she was 'safe'. What chaos! (And how glad I was to be celibate for a while. . . .)

One other point about our early, shambolic experimentation with the rhythm method. These days, it's often claimed that females who live in large communities together (nurses' homes, boarding schools and so on) very soon start menstruating *all at the same time*.

From our experiences at that time, I can say with reasonable assurance that this is nonsense. The menstrual cycles of the sexually-active occupants of our nurses' home differed wildly from one another – and the more Lothario-like members of the medical school seemed to be forever scanning pocket diaries in a very worried way – to ascertain who was 'due' today, and who (they hoped) wasn't due until next week.

*   *   *

You may well ask why all these free-loving young ladies weren't on the Pill. In fact, although it had been invented about seven years previously, its use was still almost unknown in Britain. People sometimes blame the Pill for the coming of the permissive society (if you'll forgive the phrase); but, in reality, while the permissive society more or less began to get going in about 1963, the Pill wasn't used on a *really* wide scale till about 1970. (I first remember prescribing it in 1968: the lady in question promptly developed a clot on her lungs and nearly died. I had great difficulty in persuading her to stop taking it.)

What about the coil (or IUD)? This too was virtually unknown in the Britain of the early 1960s, though us final year students were aware that some such device had been developed by a German doctor many years before. An English consultant had described it as 'the illegal and immoral invention of a foreign criminal'! Of all those pejorative words, the one that was most condemnatory was probably 'foreign'.

A few medical students tried buying vaginal contraceptive foam but, as Alan remarked, 'It makes you feel as if you're fighting a fire, really.' Also, it wasn't very safe.

That left the cap (the diaphragm) which, as I mentioned earlier, was the only method of contraception we'd had a lecture on. Unfortunately, it really wasn't a practical proposition for the nurses and physios who made up most of our girl-friends – for the simple reason that, in the 1960s, most family planning clinics (where such things were to be obtained) generally refused to see anyone who wasn't married. You stood a chance if you wore a Woolworth's wedding ring.

No wonder that so many of the final year medics were in such a state of emotional muddle as they approached their qualifying exams. And, though it seems almost incredible now, a few of them were still relying on one of the oldest, dottiest and most completely useless methods of protection against unwanted pregnancy: *getting their sweethearts to sit up and give a big cough at the instant of climax!*

Can you imagine anything sillier and more unromantic? At the very instant when the couple were supposed to be feeling at their most impassioned, most close and, one hopes, most loving, the gallant young gent (due to become a qualified doctor in a few months!) would yell out, 'Quick, darling – sit up and *cough*!'

It was more like testing for a hernia than making love.

*　　　*　　　*

So, we studied even harder during the last year: when we weren't sitting in on clinics or attending ward rounds or going to lectures, we were endlessly, endlessly 'flogging the books' – usually well into the small hours of the morning.

It may seem surprising to you that we still had *more* subjects to study. But after all, the public rather optimistically expects doctors to be absolutely omniscient on every medical topic from transplant surgery to Freudian analysis. So, we just had to plough on trying to absorb subject after subject as best we could.

What subjects? Well, first there was paediatrics – which is, of course, the study of children and their illnesses.

It was totally fascinating, and the patients were naturally delightful – making a welcome change from the aggressive, demanding and querulous adults who (I'm very sorry to say) made up quite a chunk of the hospital's clientele. I rapidly came to appreciate that kids are almost never neurotic – a curious thing really, when one considers that by the age of twenty at least a fifth of us have started showing *decidedly* neurotic symptoms!

Childhood illnesses were taught by Sir William Sheldrake, who was paediatrician to the Royal Family. We were, of course, deeply impressed by the fact that this elegant man, always dressed in black jacket and striped trousers, frequently had to cancel ward rounds in order to go and see the young Prince Charles or Princess Anne. More importantly, he was a fine teacher from whom I learned the One Great Secret of examining children: don't alarm them by making a great fuss at them.

Again and again, I watched as wild and squalling youngsters were brought into his consulting room. For the first five minutes or so, he would completely ignore them, letting them rampage around the room as they wished, while he talked in a very soft and gentle voice with the mother. At the end of this time, nearly all of them would have given up bawling or chasing around, and were completely happy to be examined by this intriguing old gentleman with the gold glasses.

Doubtless Prince Charles and Princess Anne felt the same trust in him, but for reasons of professional confidence, he did not, of course, communicate with us on that point.

*   *   *

One of the big attractions about paediatrics was that it was easy to see that, in a high proportion of cases, Sir William and his staff *were able to make the kids better*. For once the script which we'd learned in childhood ('Doctors are people who make you better . . .') was agreeably accurate. It was enormously rewarding to see a child brought into the ward gasping his little life away with pneumonia – and to see the same child a few hours later, well on the road to recovery thanks to good nursing and a carefully chosen antibiotic.

But there was a down-side to paediatrics, and it was this: I found it very hard to understand how a supposedly loving Creator killed so many children – often in such obscene and cruel ways.

I must admit that the deaths of children and the suffering of children helped, at about this time, to make me lose my faith. *Why* should a beautiful, innocent child get cancer or leukaemia? (And, in those days, the diagnosis of leukaemia was an invariable death sentence.)

Similarly, why should so many parents find out – too late – that they were carrying genes which made it all too likely that their children would be crippled, deformed or doomed to short, painful, distress-filled lives?

I remember one particularly decent father and mother who had two daughters. As is so often the case, these girls had seemed well as babies, but then the first one developed a dreadful disease of the nervous system and the lungs. Slowly, she became wobbly, uncoordinated and helpless. Her chest was frequently so filled with fluid that every breath was a fight for life.

And then, of course, the couple's worst fears came true: the younger girl developed the disease too. Though they devoted themselves selflessly to both daughters, the mother and father must now have guessed that what lay ahead was a long double agony – to be ended only by both girls' deaths.

Having seen the family while I was a student, I actually looked after the girls a year or two later when I was a qualified doctor. The elder daughter was on her last legs by then, the younger one very nearly so.

Yet the father and mother still had great hope. They maintained a conviction that a Dr Ponsonby (who worked at another teaching hospital some miles away) had 'special knowledge' of this disease, and so would be able to save the girls – if he could only be persuaded to come over and see them.

With my chief's permission, I rang Dr Ponsonby and he agreed to visit the ward. I thought it was very decent of him to put himself out like that and, carried away a bit by the patients' hopes, I waited excitedly for his arrival – half-expecting that he would indeed have some secret new cure concealed about his person.

I met him when he stepped out of the lift, and was rather disappointed to see a pompous, youngish, and slightly shifty-looking man, rather than the brilliant researcher I'd imagined. Still, as we entered the ward I thanked him for coming over.

'Not at all,' he said in a stage whisper. 'The reason I'm here is that as soon as these kids die, I want to get their hearts as fresh as possible for my research project. So here's my private phone number: will you ring me the moment they cough it?'

I felt appalled – though with hindsight, I suppose I was wrong. Although he had no cure to offer the parents, and had simply come to make sure he got the girls' hearts, his mere arrival must have given them some hope and confidence. And, after all, it was just possible that the *post-mortem* research which he was doing might eventually lead to a cure for the disease. But it hasn't yet.

Both girls died a few months afterwards, though I had moved to another job by then. But I'm sure that my successor arranged for their hearts to be removed instantly and sent across London to the research lab. I hope the parents understood.

*   *   *

On a more cheerful note, our final year was enlivened by the study of VD.

You may not think that venereal diseases constitute a very happy subject, but they do really – mainly because nearly all of them are so *curable*. (Of course, we didn't have AIDS in the 1960s – and herpes was very rare indeed.)

And the other nice thing about this speciality was that you could cheer people up so rapidly! You see, most of the patients who *thought* they'd got VD turned out either:
(a) to have nothing wrong with them at all; or
(b) to have some fairly minor and non-venereal malady – like vaginal thrush, for instance.
And of those who *did* have VD, at least ninety-nine per cent could be told right away that they'd be cured very shortly.

You can appreciate that it's immensely agreeable to be able to reassure worried people in that way. And to say that the patients were worried is a heck of an understatement! When they first arrived at the hospital, many of them were so jittery that they accidentally stumbled into our refectory – which, through an interesting piece of planning, had been put next to the VD department.

So, we soon grew used to the fact that, as we sat at our

lunch, munching our Spam fritters or our spotted dick
(a curiously venereological dish that, I've always felt),
we'd be furtively approached by agonised-looking chaps
who, noticing a white coat, would sidle up and whisper in
one's ear, 'Excuse me, doc: could you please direct me to
Z-Block?'

Many of the men had clearly been convinced by popular
folklore that their knobs were going to drop off at any
moment. The women, on the other hand, were understandably terrified at the prospect of being made infertile, and
were often deeply distressed at what they regarded as the
'dirtiness' and shame of the whole business.

It struck me very forcibly that it would be nice to be able
to allay the panic and embarrassment of these poor men
and women. That was one of the reasons why, a decade or
so later, I took up the speciality of VD for a period of some
years.

You may well feel that spending one's time inspecting
people's cocks and gazing up their crumpets constitutes an
odd way of making a living. But I suspect that out of all
those physicians who claim to be relieving human anxiety
and suffering, the 'pox doctors' must deserve to be
somewhere near the top of the league.

One other curious thing about VD: for some strange
reason, nearly all of us students firmly believed that we
were immune to it! Sexually-transmitted diseases were
things that were caught by other folk, and which couldn't
possibly affect *us*.

That is, of course, the same daft ostrich-like attitude
which we see so often among the young (and indeed the
old) in the Nervous Nineties of the AIDS era.

Anyway, the general feeling among my friends that we
were totally safe from sexually-transmitted disease lasted
until about a year after we qualified – when a wildly
promiscuous nurse decided to set about the remarkable
(and remarkably silly) feat of seducing every houseman in
the hospital. She was about half-way through this long,

though not over-difficult, enterprise when one thing became appallingly clear to all those who had already succumbed to her charms.

She had crabs! And, alas, even doctors are not immune to *them*.

*   *   *

When we came to study psychiatric illnesses, there was (once again) a feeling that *that* sort of thing didn't happen to chaps like us, did it?

In our stiff-upper-lip medical culture, emotional illness was something that happened to *patients*. Still, the fact that the subject of psychiatry was taught to us at all was a considerable advance. Not long before our time, medical students had simply been given six of what were called 'loony lectures' – and that was it! This was quite bizarre when you consider just how much of medical practice consists in dealing with people's emotions.

But by the 1960s, our medical school had had the sense to start a long course of lectures on the workings of the human mind, delivered by a superb teacher called Sir Dennis Will. An extraordinarily entertaining and wily old cove, he taught us something that I've never seen in any work of popular psychology: that there are certain clearly-defined human personality traits which we all possess – and which, if they become exaggerated by stress and strain, will develop into a full-blown neurosis.

They include obsessionalism, hysteria, and anxiety.

Let's just look at obsessionalism for a moment. You or I like life to be fairly reasonably ordered; we like to 'know where we are'; we like our homes to be sufficiently tidy for us to find things when we want them. And, deep down, we probably have some little 'obsessive' rituals – like organising our desks or dressing tables in a particular way; or perhaps praying at a special time of day; or regularly touching wood for luck; or, in the case of many children, always trying to avoid stepping on the lines in the pavement.

But a large chunk of the population is far more obsessive than that. They want everything to be 'just so' all the time. Meticulous, neat, pedantic, thorough and (almost always!) *totally* obsessed with the regularity of their own bowels, they can be a thorough nuisance to more easy-going folk.

However . . . these are the people who ensure that so many things in our society *actually work* – they plan extremely thoroughly; they do their best to make everything run on time; they insist on strict standards of hygiene; they repair things meticulously and well; they run businesses and civil service departments with martinet-like efficiency; they make marvellous 'daily helps'; they compile thoroughly reliable lists and indexes and they see to it that books like this are (of course) totally free of punctuation errors and spelling mistakes! So we *need* obsessive people – difficult though they may be to live with at times.

Unfortunately, when an obsessive person is under some stress, things get out of hand, and an 'obsessional neurosis' may well develop. If this happens, the victim is completely overcome by his or her need for precision, neatness, cleanliness and ritual. So, a government minister suddenly finds that he has to line up 200 paper-clips on his desk before he can start the day's business; a student finds that he cannot study unless he repeats the Lord's Prayer every five minutes on the dot; a housewife finds that she is compelled to wash her hands 200 times a day 'to protect her family against germs'.

Fortunately, care and understanding and a reduction in stress will bring many of these people out of their neurosis – and back to being their usual meticulous and very useful selves.

I was amazed to find that I knew so many mildly obsessional people – including, for instance, fellow-students who kept neat, beautifully-written notes of absolutely everything we were taught, and who *had* to go to the loo at seven o'clock each morning.

But slowly I realised, thanks to Sir Dennis, that there's a

little bit of obsessionalism (and of the other personality traits) in each and every one of us.

Pardon me just a moment, will you? It's just that I always trim my nails on a Thursday.

*   *   *

Though the professor of psychiatry was a superb communicator, he managed to give medical students throughout the country one of the grossest pieces of misinformation about female sexuality one could possibly imagine.

In the great medical textbook which most of us used (I have my copy in front of me right now), he announced for some reason that *'twenty-five per cent of women are constitutionally frigid.'*

Such a view, may I say, was pretty widespread at the time. So, the medics of the 1960s went out into the world as doctors, having been told in a textbook by one of Britain's most famous psychiatrists that a quarter of all females are 'frigid'!

Those students who found this statement to be totally contrary to their own social experience may perhaps have been driven to doubt the absolute infallibility of professors of psychiatry.

Or maybe they just reckoned that so far they'd really been jolly lucky. . . .

*   *   *

Somewhere fairly late in the final year, somebody decided to teach first aid (though it's doubtful whether this was strictly necessary, in view of the bloodbath that we'd all been through in Casualty).

The first-aid course consisted of one lecture, given by a nice consultant anaesthetist who wasn't actually involved at all in first aid himself. The advice he gave us was astounding.

'The St John Ambulance and the Red Cross know all about first aid, chaps. So it's best to leave it to them, really.

Now you'll find when you qualify that nurses and people are always ringing you up and shrieking at you to come *at once*, because somebody's dying. Well, I assure you, boys, there's *never* any point in rushing to an emergency. In general, patients either die or they don't. So when someone tells you to come quick, my advice to you is to walk around the block a couple of times and smoke your pipe first.'

A clarion call indeed I think you'll agree. Still, times have changed.

*   *   *

The mention of 'smoking your pipe' may strike you as rather surprising – but in the 60s, many doctors and medical students still smoked like chimneys.

This was largely because of a widespread feeling (fostered by the highly-effective propaganda campaign of the tobacco industry, and backed by certain newspapers who depended on cigarette advertising) that 'the case against smoking wasn't really *proven* yet.'

But of course, it was. Late in our course we were fortunate enough to be taught chest medicine by Dr Phillip Hughes-Evans – a clever pulmonary specialist who really stood out as a fine lecturer.

In a matter of an hour, Hughes-Evans deployed the full force of his arguments to demonstrate to us beyond doubt that smoking was ruinous for the lungs, and that furthermore it was clearly the main cause of the dreadful disease which was killing 30,000 people a year: lung cancer. He also demonstrated to us that if you *gave up*, you could still save yourself.

His logic was quite irrefutable. In the course of that sixty minutes, I believe that he probably turned several dozen medical students into lifelong non-smokers. Including me.

I went home and tried to convince my favourite uncle, who was a forty-a-day man. He's the bloke to whom this book is dedicated: Freddy Hoar, a lovely chap who'd taught me as a child about the glories of English literature, and who had brought some civilisation to my rather turbulent Celtic upbringing.

Now this was a bloke who was far above average intelligence; he'd done well at Oxford and was Head of English at a large grammar school. Yet, like most smokers, he deluded himself completely about the dangers of cigarettes. So, he listened courteously to what I had to say about smoking, and then – equally courteously – rejected my advice. You see, apparently, a man in a pub had explained to him that 'the doctors have made a statistical mistake.'

Oh really? Yes – it appeared that when 'the doctors' had found that most of the people who die of lung cancer are smokers, *they'd forgotten to allow for the fact that most people are smokers anyway*. Pretty convincing argument, eh?

My uncle's brain loved the nicotine, and I suppose that was why I couldn't convince him that the Regius Professor of Medicine at Oxford (who'd been mainly responsible for demonstrating that cigarettes caused carcinoma) didn't make childish statistical mistakes like that one. So, Freddy carried on smoking.

Six years later, he was dead. Of lung cancer.

* * *

I think you'll have seen from this chapter (and from a lot of what has gone before) that among the biggest influences in a young doctor's training are *the consultants who teach him*.

I was readily impressed by brilliant communicators like Phillip Hughes-Evans, David Codd, and Professor Sir Dennis Will, and I carry with me for life much of what they said (though *not* the bit about twenty-five per cent of ladies being frigid!).

But, unfortunately, we had by now soaked up one or two rather unpleasant attitudes from some of our consultants. I mean their arrogance, their snobbery, and their disdainful refusal to discuss anything with their patients.

Why did they set us this poor example? Partly, I suppose, it was due to their 'Harley Street syndrome': if you're a consultant who has fought his way to the very top of the ladder of British medicine by treading down your rivals; if you've made a good deal of money in the buccaneering world of private practice; if you've equipped yourself with the symbolic trappings of consultanthood, like a Rolls-Royce or a Bentley; if you always wear those wildly impressive dark suits which we used to call 'consultoid' – well, it's then quite difficult to lower yourself sufficiently to have a friendly chat with Mrs Bloggs, the road-mender's wife. Some consultants could do it; many couldn't.

In fairness, there was another factor which made it difficult for them to communicate with their patients (and vice versa). That factor was the very big gap in intelligence between them and so many of their patients.

Perhaps you don't like that comment? Well, nowadays a lot of people seem to be offended by the simple statement that some folk are bright, while others aren't. But it's true, of course.

Have a look at this illustration, which shows you how IQ is distributed among the population.

DISTRIBUTION OF I.Q. IN THE POPULATION

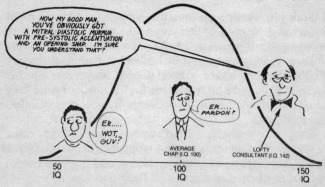

As you can see, it's a bowler hat-shaped curve – with most of the population being somewhere near the 100 mark, and a very few people being over 150 (extremely bright) or under 50 (very badly sub-normal).

However, the average teaching hospital consultant is located somewhere about where I've put the black arrow on the chart – not quite Mensa material, perhaps, but so far above the average that there are many times when he's talking to patients who, quite literally, have half his IQ. Even the average chap is thirty or forty points down on him.

This doesn't exactly make for easy communication about complex matters of medicine, *unless* the consultant is willing to try really hard to make himself intelligible to his patients! But if, as so often happens, you have a consultant who has grown up in the rigid, hierarchical teaching hospital structure that I've tried to describe in this book, there's a fairly high chance that he won't even *try* to use clear, simple phrases which the ordinary punter can understand.

That's why we still have patients who go into hospital, undergo very serious operations – and then come out having not the remotest idea of what has been done to them. Once or twice during my final year, I even ran into chaps who'd had major operations and who, when I asked them what the surgeons had done, replied, 'Oh, they just took away *everything*, doc. The lot.'

An interesting concept: it seemed to these poor blokes that the consultant surgeon had merely gone in and taken out ALL the internal organs, leaving nothing but a vast and trouble-free space inside the body.

Would that life were so simple.

*   *   *

Another thing which made communication with patients so difficult was the fact that by now we spoke a very different language from them.

Very soon after we'd started on the wards, it had become clear to us that doctors actually had a special dialect – not just a minor variant of Upper Middle Class English, but a genuine dialect in which there were many hundreds of words and phrases and abbreviations not normally used in British speech (words like 'neoplasm', 'metaplastic', 'polymorphic', 'cryptogenic', 'iatrogenic' and 'overlay'. By the time we were in our final year, we were really adept at this jargon, and could easily hold a conversation at the foot of a patient's bed without the poor guy having the faintest idea of what we were talking about.

I don't mean that this 'doctors' dialect' had ever been deliberately thought up for the purpose of deceiving patients: it's more a sort of specialist lingo that's grown up over the centuries. But, as you can probably imagine, it was often used in a *kindly* way to spare patients from the fright of realising that we were actually discussing cancer as a possible diagnosis. (We learned that there were literally dozens of esoteric words which the consultants could use in order to let us know that cancer was at least being considered.)

Less pleasantly, though perhaps understandably, it was extremely common for our chiefs to use the jargon in order to tell us that the patient in front of us was a neurotic, and that his or her symptoms could therefore be disregarded. The key jargon words indicating this opinion would then probably get inscribed on his medical notes for the rest of his life.

By this final year, we found that we talked among ourselves all the time in this trade lingo – and indeed most of us would continue to use it for the rest of our careers. When I meet another doctor and chat to her or him about medicine, I instinctively fall into this fast, throwaway dialect – which everyone else, except possibly a nurse, or an outstandingly clever Greek and Latin scholar, would find immensely hard to understand. (That's why no medical novel or film or TV programme *ever* reproduces doctors' conversation correctly: the readers/viewers just wouldn't be able to understand it.)

To give you an example, I remember standing at the foot of a bed and talking to a mate of mine – another fifth-year student – about a chap who we'd both just examined. Suddenly I said to Mike, 'Of course, we have to bear in mind that the mutual ethanol concentration is zero milogrammes per cent at the moment.'

Without hesitation, he replied, 'Anethanolaemia? Well, that should be corrected, shouldn't it? When would it be possible for the fluid balance to be restored?'

I glanced at my watch and replied 'Stat' – and we immediately wished a slightly surprised patient 'Good-evening' and departed.

What we'd told each other was that we both fancied a drink – and the hospital pub had just opened.

I'm sorry if you're a bit shocked that the hospital had its own little pub for the doctors and students. Yes, there were periods when we spent too much time (and money) there. But we wouldn't be using it very much in the immediate future – because the last dreadful hurdle of the qualifying exams was now almost on us.

13

QUALIFYING

THE FIRST MEDICAL examination I ever remember taking was called a 'spot exam'.

No, it *didn't* involve going round and looking at people's pimples. It was designed to test your anatomical knowledge of various spots (i.e., places) in the body, and how it worked was this.

You stood outside the examination room door, tensely waiting for somebody inside to hit a bell. The moment it rang, you charged in and dashed to the first of twenty numbered tables.

On each table was something about six inches (fifteen centimetres) across that looked like a reject joint of meat from the local butchers. It was, however, a small lump of dead human being. A coloured pin was sticking out of it, and a piece of white card alongside the lump invited the gallant medical student to name the nerve, artery or vein in which it was stuck.

You had one minute to do this; then the bell was struck again, and you moved on to the second of the twenty tables (just as the next candidate came flying through the entry door behind you).

The whole fairly ghastly process took exactly twenty minutes – and, at the end of it, I'd got about five specimens right, which gave me a mark of twenty-five per cent. Gulp!

However, all that had been five years previously, and my academic record had improved a good deal since then, thank heavens.

In fact, just as we were about to embark on the final exams that would, with luck, make us into doctors, I sat the hospital's own prize examinations and was lucky enough to win three of them – including the one I wanted most: the prize in psychological medicine.

However, I did *not* win the prize for tropical diseases – having rather unwisely entered the exam. room wearing a colonial-style sun helmet. (I think they thought I was taking the pith.)

All of this should, I suppose, have given me some confidence for taking Finals. But it didn't, really – partly because I knew they were going to be such a prolonged ordeal. Looking at my diary for that year, I find that they dragged on for *ten months*!

Also, I didn't start out on those ten months in the best of physical shape. You see, four weeks before the exams began, I very unwisely played yet another game of rugby. A devastating tackle from an opposing centre three-quarter left me helpless on the ground, knowing that I'd broken my left leg.

With a sinking feeling, I realised as I lay there in the mud that I had just a month to get myself mobile enough to struggle into the exam. room.

On the credit side, the ref was *most* impressed by my instant diagnosis, and felt certain that I had a great medical career ahead of me! *Very* reassuring, you'll agree. . . .

*   *   *

Now I forgot to tell you why our Finals were going to go on for so long. It wasn't just that there were loads of different subjects which we had to be examined in; there was another, more bizarre reason.

You see, in England there are three possible ways in which a medical student can qualify as a doctor:

- There's his university degree – which is (naturally) pretty hard. They give you a very small, but much cherished, certificate if you pass the university exams.
- There's also an optional set of qualifying examinations run jointly by the Royal Colleges of Proctology and Pedostomatology. These are a bit easier, but they cost you more money to enter – and you're given a really BIG diploma if you pass.
- Finally, there are the exams set by a medieval City of London guild known as the Worshipful Society of Leeches. The Worshipful Society hold their examinations very frequently indeed, and they charge a lot of money to those who want to enter them. But their exams aren't very difficult to pass. And they give you a HUGE diploma if you can qualify as a doctor in this way!

There used to be a fourth possible method of qualifying – which involved crossing the Irish Sea for a few days, handing over a sizeable sum of cash, and answering some undemanding questions at an institute known as Apothecaries' Hall. Alas, *that* agreeably Celtic route to becoming a doctor was banned by my colleagues on the GMC some years ago. (A pity, because it did wonders for the Irish tourist trade. . . .)

Anyway, the point is this: most of us thought it wiser to sit one of the 'soft' qualifications, as well as taking our university degree exams – in case we failed the latter. The result was that we were taking various examining bodies' examinations in various subjects, week after week, month after month, with (I can assure you) enormous stress piled on enormous stress throughout that year.

Some chaps actually sat the exams for all THREE possible ways of qualifying. If they were eventually successful, then they'd find that at the age of twenty-two or twenty-three they'd already have a wallful of impressive-looking diplomas, plus the right to put after their names the following astonishing collection of letters:

M.B., B.Ch., L.R.C.P., M.R.C.S. (ENGLAND),
L.M.S.S.A. (LONDON).

(There's actually a Scottish qualification which gives you even more letters, but we won't go into that.)

For the rest of their lives, the public – seeing this string of initials – would regard these blokes as incredibly well-qualified 'specialists'. In reality, of course, they have nothing more than basic qualifications which indicate that they are doctors. (This is one of the great private jokes of British medicine.)

Incidentally, we all believed fervently that through ancient lore, one of the above sets of qualifications entitles a doctor to:

wear a sword in the City of London;

drive a flock of sheep across Tower Bridge;

relieve himself behind the wheel of his carriage within the sound of Bow bells.

So far, I haven't had the nerve to risk any of them. But you never know. . . .

*   *   *

OK – so now I had to face it, broken leg and all. Actually, it hadn't really been a very serious break, and I was off crutches and limping around with a walking stick by the time the exam in the first subject began.

It was held in a vast examination hall located in Queen Square, London, conveniently next to the National Hospital for Nervous Diseases. That first subject was internal medicine (which means lung and heart and kidney disease and so on), and – like most medical exams – it was divided into three phases:

Written papers;

Viva voces (i.e., face-to-face interviews);

Practical.

On the first day, I hobbled up the great stairs, fortified by a few aspirin, and ploughed through the initial written papers; they were about recognising coronaries, treating chronic bronchitis, and diagnosing kidney failure.

They were difficult, but at least (with still-fresh recollections of my mother's last illness in my mind) I didn't have too much of a problem with the one on kidney trouble.

Once the written papers were over, we returned another day for the *viva voces*, in which we would be grilled across an interview table.

There was something endearingly typical of British medicine about the way the *vivas* were organised. The consultants who did the interviewing all wore beautiful Harley Street suits, often with a rose or carnation in the button-hole. And it was made quite clear that we were expected to imitate them in sartorial style – at least, as far as our pockets would permit.

So, any boy who was mad enough to turn up in a sports jacket was doomed. (Yes, *doomed*.) A smart suit was *de rigueur*, and a discreet college tie or bow tie was a wise precaution. A waistcoat with a watch-chain across it (even if there was no watch on the end of it) was widely reckoned to be worth a couple of extra marks.

The bell inside the examination room rang, and I pushed my way through the glass doors, full of trepidation and tripping over my walking-stick.

I limped towards two of the gods of the medical profession, who were sitting side by side at a couple of old-fashioned desks.

'Good heavens! What happened to *you*?' exclaimed one of them.

I sat down and (for some odd reason) slotted my walking-stick through the empty ink-well hole on his desk. I could see he was surprised by this – as well he might be. So I launched into an explanation of my injury, complete with graphic details of how the rugby match had gone up till the moment of the fracture.

Being physicians, they knew nothing at all about broken bones, so they merely clucked away sympathetically till I'd finished. Much to my relief, I found that there was by now very little time left for this particular *viva*. Once we'd got my rugby injury out of the way, the two of them asked me a few straightforward questions about heart failure and the drugs used to treat it – and then the bell pinged again and it was off to the next pair of examiners.

They were *not* terribly impressed by my Long John Silver appearance, and proceeded to grill me intensively about the complications of mumps. (I wasn't really expecting this, since I thought it was part of paediatrics.)

But, fortunately, I was fairly well up in the complications of that particular ailment, mainly because I was terrified of one of them (inflamed testicles). So, the examiners and I happily patted little bits of knowledge about mumps to and fro across the desk till the bell rang again.

Things continued like that for the rest of the *viva* session. I limped from table to table, wishing each pair of interrogators 'Good-morning, sir; good-morning, sir.' I sat up straight (as we had been taught), and I always said at the close of each interview: 'Thank you, sir; thank you, sir.'

I don't claim that the strict observation of these points of etiquette was more important than the actual answers we gave – but, like the correct choice of clothes, it certainly helped.

So, we dressed and behaved in the same conservative way a week or two later when along came the practical exams – in the same subject of internal medicine.

What does the word 'practical' mean? Well, the big examination hall was now filled with beds, surrounded by screens. In the beds were various patients who'd been selected from the wards of the teaching hospitals as 'interesting material'. Lured by the prospect of a day out plus a small fee, they'd apparently agreed to come up to Queen Square and have would-be doctors examine them.

The general idea was that we'd be given a few minutes with one patient (a 'short case') and would then be grilled by an examiner on what we'd found; then we'd do another couple of short cases in the same way; and finally we'd have a 'long case', with whom we could spend half an hour.

As usual with medical examinations, the whole thing was governed by those blasted shop bells; an acolyte struck one to kick things off, and we'd charge into the room and make for our first 'short case'; four minutes later he'd clout the clanger again, and we were off and running to the next bed. (Thank heavens, I'd discarded my walking-stick by now.) The patients, to their credit, mostly regarded this medicated steeple-chase with good-natured amusement.

My first short case patient was a dream – for me, at least, though not for him. He was a middle-aged black man who looked healthy enough; but I put my hand on his belly and felt the hard spleen underneath my fingertips. When the examiner asked me the diagnosis, I told him (in our carefully coded language) that it was probably leukaemia.

'That's good,' he replied. The bell rang, and I moved on – leaving behind a man who, since there was no curative treatment in those days, would be dead within six months.

As far as I remember, there then came a bloke with a rare nerve disorder which gives you legs shaped like champagne bottles; I blundered around, near enough to the diagnosis to get by.

Finally, the bell rang to start me on my all-important long case – in which I would have thirty minutes to take a complete history from a patient, and then examine him or her completely.

I stepped behind the screens and found to my horror that the patient in question was a very senile old lady. Perhaps her wits had been brighter when the long day had started, but now she was completely incapable of giving that vital history. All I could get out of her was something about being breathless.

My heart was in my boots, and when I examined *her* heart, it wasn't in great shape either. But apart from that, half an hour's examination of her poor old body gave me almost no positive information at all.

When the examiner came in and asked me for my diagnosis, I knew I was in desperate trouble. I told him what I'd found and nervously suggested that she might have a certain disorder in which lung disease (characterised by breathlessness) causes problems with the heart. It's called *cor pulmonale*, but I felt as though I might as well have said 'Cor blimey'!

His face betrayed no reaction at all – in fact, he was slightly less communicative than the patient. He then asked me a series of what sounded like sarcastic questions, about how I would treat the old lady.

I fended them off as best I could, at least managing to have the sense not to suggest powerful drugs or other dramatic remedies. I tried (by speaking in impressive-sounding phrases like 'treating the patient conservatively') to give the impression that I had a wise seventy-two-year-old head on twenty-two-year-old shoulders. Alas, I felt pretty certain that the examiner was not impressed.

The bell rang for the last time, and he curtly dismissed me.

I went sadly home with a mate of mine, knowing that I must have failed this section of the exams; I would certainly have to sit it all again in six months' time.

A week later, a typed postcard from the examining body arrived through my letter-box. I'd passed.

*   *   *

The next chunk of Finals concerned gynaecology, on which I seemed to do a bit better. I'm not being rude when I say that I always seemed to have a much clearer idea about disorders of the vagina than I did about the diseases of the more esoteric bits of the bile duct or the inner ear.

I wore a bow tie for the gynae *viva* and so did the chief examiner, which seemed to help. Rightly or wrongly, there was no 'practical' – presumably because no woman would have been mad enough to come up to London and let herself be examined internally once every four minutes, as soon as a bell rang.

The second postcard soon arrived, and it said that I'd passed the gynaecology part of the Finals too. What relief!

But there was *no* relief really, because as the spring and summer came and went, we were trapped on an endless conveyor belt of revision and ward rounds and clinics and more revision.

One night I took a break from flogging the books and went to a party. I met a tall, dark-haired and staggeringly beautiful nurse, and danced and flirted and kissed with her all evening.

It was one of those medical student parties which went on till it was too late for the girls to get back into the nurses' home. So the beautiful, statuesque nurse spent the night in my arms on a settee – but totally chastely, since we were surrounded by some twenty other people in various stages of booziness (and envy).

Next day, she invited me to see *Boeing-Boeing* that night at the theatre (nurses often got free West End tickets). We went to the show, and during the course of the evening this lovely creature made it quite clear that she was willing to give herself to me when we got back.

Worried sick by the turmoil of the exams, I simply took her to the door of the nurses' home and bade her good-night without even kissing her.

She must have thought I was completely mad.

*   *   *

Very soon, we were back at Queen Square for another battle with the examiners on yet another subject: pathology.

Pathology really covers the 'laboratory' aspects of medicine, and I did *not* consider myself too brilliant at it. But at least I was getting used to travelling to Examination Hall now – used to coming out of the tube station at Russell Square, and used to wandering eastwards past a pub called the Friend At Hand (in which, if it was lunchtime, a number of the gallant candidates would be fuelling themselves with pre-exam Dutch courage). The sign outside the pub depicted a drowning sailor (which more or less summed up what I felt about pathology). But there was at least a lifeboatman on the horizon, who might pull him out of the drink. With luck.

When I got to the examination hall in Queen Square for the pathology practical, I made as usual for the gents, in order to have an anxious pre-practical pee (quite difficult to say that – and quite difficult to do at the time, owing to my general state of exam nerves). But I was astonished to find that the officials were making all of us young gentlemen pass water into large funnels – from which lengths of rubber tubing conducted our urine into huge and rather repellent-looking glass jars.

Was this part of the exam? You may well ask – but the answer is 'no'. For I gradually twigged that what was happening was that we were expected to provide the basic material for the practical; our urine would be taken upstairs, a few lumps of sugar would be thrown into it, and then we'd be asked to test it for diabetes.

Extraordinary. The cold-hearted pathologists who'd set the practical clearly saw no reason to go to the expense of 'buying in' large quantities of urine, since the candidates could provide it themselves.

I'm only surprised they didn't expect us to supply the basic *matériel* for the blood and sperm tests too – though, in most cases, we'd have been far, far too fraught to provide the latter.

*   *   *

I staggered slightly indignantly, but successfully, through the pathology section of Finals, and got ready for the next onslaught.

At this stage, we were due to be examined in something called 'surgical anatomy', so we were desperately mugging up all the dissection work we'd done four or five years back. To my intense relief, I found that the positions of the thousands of muscles, nerves, bones, tendons, ligaments and blood vessels seemed to have stuck in my head moderately well, and so I managed to scrape through.

While sitting this subject at an overseas medical school, a friend of mine discovered that he would be expected to perform a full surgical operation on a corpse! Having spent weeks revising all sorts of complicated and delicate abdominal operations, he was relieved to find that all he had to do in order to pass was to remove the poor old body's kneecap – which is a brutal but quite easy business.

In London, our surgical anatomy exam was rather less dramatic. The practical section simply involved selecting a surgical instrument from a pile, naming it and saying what you would do with it.

Like most students, I played safe and selected a simple pair of forceps. However, my gifted friend Mike Beall surveyed the pile of ironmongery on the green baize table, rummaged a while among it – and then produced a weird and complicated-looking instrument which no candidate had ever chosen before.

'What is *that*?' enquired a surprised examiner.

'That, sir, is Sir St Clair Thompson's adenoidal curette.'

Mike went on to explain how the strange instrument had been invented by Sir St Clair Thompson in order to enable him to stick it into the upper reaches of the throats of refractory infants, and thus to scrape their adenoids away (privately, of course).

The examiners, who found themselves in the odd position of knowing far less about the subject than the candidate did, posed the inevitable question 'Who was Sir St Clair Thompson?'

Mike gravely explained that Sir St Clair had been one of the great society ear, nose and throat surgeons of forty years before. As a young and newly-qualified man, St Clair had of course been quite unknown. But he had hit upon the quite brilliant idea of dining every evening at very fashionable London restaurants, like the Savoy and Claridge's. After many months, the opportunity he had been waiting for arrived at last. In Wheeler's one night, a sprig of the aristocracy choked briefly on a fish-bone. St Clair was on him in a flash, crying out 'Stand back – I am an ENT surgeon!'

He bore the unfortunate son of a duke to the floor and, whipping out the scalpel which he always kept ready in his tails, carried out an emergency tracheotomy. (It was a pity he couldn't have used the adenoidal curette really, wasn't it?) An ambulance was summoned, and the patient was carted off to a private clinic, with St Clair at his side (or at his throat).

Thompson's reputation in London's *beau monde* was thus established, and fame, fortune and a knighthood were soon his. His story was in some ways a model to which all ambitious young surgeons might aspire. . . .

Years later, I discovered that this story of Mike's was pure hokum. Sir St Clair Thompson was indeed a fine ENT surgeon who'd invented the adenoidal curette – but he is not known to have done a tracheotomy in Wheeler's and his 'knighthood' (i.e., being called 'Sir') was in fact a baronetcy, and therefore inherited from his Dad.

Nonetheless, the examiners awarded Mike Honours in his Final exams. And quite right too.

* * *

After much trauma, we eventually arrived at the last subject: general surgery. If I passed this, I would be a doctor. I made my way through the papers as calmly as possible, trying to write tolerable essays on subjects like gastric ulcers and diverticular disease of the bowel. The surgery *vivas*, I felt, went reasonably well, thanks primarily to the fact that I'd saved up and bought myself a rather classy three-piece suit to appear in.

Now there only remained the practical exam. Once again, it would be a series of short cases (punctuated by dinging bells), followed by a long one.

For the very last time, I charged in through the double doors with the bell's tinkle ringing in my ears. I sped round the short cases, diagnosing little lumps and bumps with surprising confidence.

Then came the long case. I was left alone with a lady of fifty-five or so, who lay on a couch round which the screens had been *not* very well drawn – so that with her blanket down around her waist, she was rather badly exposed to the eyes of all the other people in the vast room.

I did my best to remedy this, and asked her to tell me about her problem, which (it soon emerged) was concerned with her left breast.

Indeed, as I took her history it began to sound more and more like the classic tale of neglected cancer of the breast which I'd heard so often before: an account of a painless lump discovered months ago – a lump which nothing had been done about till it sank its fangs into the skin. This lady's life, like so many other women's lives, had almost certainly been thrown away.

When I went to examine her breast, I found that there was no real doubt about it. Like the first breast lump I had examined so long ago, this swelling under my fingers was virtually certain to be cancerous.

It seemed rather a simple diagnosis for my long case – the case which was clearly going to pass or fail me as a doctor. But there it was: I couldn't conceive of any other diagnosis at all.

After half an hour, the examiner arrived: a grumpy old consultant surgeon who seemed to have remarkably little interest in either me or the patient.

I told him the woman's story and my findings, thinking that I was making it crystal-clear what the diagnosis was, but without actually *saying* it in front of the patient.

The examiner seemed strangely unimpressed.

'Yes?' he said testily.

'Well, that's it, sir,' I concluded.

'Nothing else?'

'Er . . . no, sir.'

What I'd totally failed to realise was that this bloke had assumed that I was so stupid that I didn't know that by far the likeliest diagnosis of a hard lump in the breast was cancer.

Just at that moment, the closing bell rang. The examiner stretched out a long bony hand and pointed across the room.

'What is the diagnosis?' he enquired.

I followed the line of his finger and saw, to my amazement, that it was pointing at a very frightened-looking female medical student who was moving nervously toward the exit door.

'What rudeness!' I thought to myself. 'Fancy asking me to make a diagnosis on a fellow-student!'

Still, there *was* something familiar about the girl's bird-like appearance and nerves-shot-to-pieces demeanour. In desperate circumstances, I thought I'd better have a plunge.

'Looks like an over-active thyroid to me, sir.'

I turned and gazed at the examiner. His face was a mixture of astonishment and contempt. He spluttered, 'But an over-active thyroid doesn't give you a lump in the breast!'

With horror I realised that he *hadn't* been pointing at the girl medical student at all – he'd just been showing me the way to the door.

'Sorry, sir. Thought you were talking about . . . er . . . another patient, sir. . . .'

I was now thirty seconds over my time, and the next candidate was waiting.

'Er . . . it's breast carcinoma, sir,' I finally mumbled (hoping that the woman hadn't caught my drift). I staggered off toward the exit door leaving the examiner sadly shaking his head.

*   *   *

I vaguely remember that for some reason they then put us all in a long narrow corridor while the marks were added up.

Eventually an official came out and explained the procedure for giving us the results. He was going to stand at the far end of the corridor (in front of a statue of Queen Victoria, as I recall), holding a large book. He would then call out each student's name in turn and we would come up and get our Final result. He began.

Incredibly, those to whom he said 'failed' had to turn round and walk back through the unsympathetic throng to find their way out.

Those to whom he said 'pass' carried on and walked round behind the statue.

I waited in the crowd for ages. I remember I was reading *Private Eye*. At long last he called out 'Delvin, D.'

I walked up, putting *Private Eye* in my pocket.

'Pass,' said the Recording Angel.

I went on round behind Queen Victoria's statue. I was a doctor.

*   *   *

Once we'd got behind the Great White Mother's Statue, nobody asked us to swear the Hippocratic Oath – just as well really, because when you actually take the trouble to *read* it, it's full of all sorts of bizarre stuff about making sure you give preferential treatment to other docs and their families. (Not what you'd expect at all, really.)

What they *did* do was line us up in a room behind the statue, read us an extract from the by-laws of the Royal College, and ask us to nod in unison if we agreed. We nodded.

The diplomas followed in the post, after we'd paid an appropriate fee. In guineas, of course.

*   *   *

So that was it. After five years of struggle and stress, I'd qualified – and so had the majority of my friends and peers.

They were, by the way, a very decent lot. If you think I've painted them in this book as a bunch of promiscuous, boozy irresponsibles, then of course you're absolutely right.

But medical students were ever thus – and they mostly remain so today. (As I was finishing writing this chapter, the *British Medical Journal* came out with a survey which shows that medics – especially *women* medics – are still, unfortunately, drinking far, far too much.)

However, I hope that my slightly dotty memoirs have shown you just *why* medical students behave as they do; it's mainly because the stresses of their training are, almost inevitably, very great indeed.

That training, as you can see, is not exactly ideal. It's short on communication skills, and rather too long on élitism (and sometimes on downright snobbery).

Still, it produces doctors who are mostly pretty good, kindly and dependable people, which is one reason why the public invariably rates doctors as number one in opinion polls. (Estate agents and politicians usually come last!)

Not *all* docs are good eggs, of course. I've known two who were convicted of murder (and one who was done for attempted murder), and at the GMC I've sat on the cases of a lot more who were minor swindlers or who liked touching up their patients' private parts. ('I'm just testing to see if you can orgasm, m'dear. . . .')

But it's still a fine profession, and I'm proud to belong to it. On that day when I qualified, I was able to look back over all the pain and the worry and the grindingly intensive work (and of course the fun), and to feel that it *had* all been worth it – for the privilege of joining a profession which genuinely does its best to heal people.

I had no idea of the bizarre way in which my career would go. I couldn't have guessed that one day I'd lead a rebel Junior Hospital Doctors' movement; or that I would practise medicine in the land of James Bond; or that I would become a rather inept medical film director, and later a 'TV doctor'; or that I'd be taken on as agony aunt by *She* magazine and, thanks to them, become for eighteen years the author of the most outrageous and uninhibited (though p'raps not the best-written) sex advice column ever to appear in a British women's journal.

I couldn't have forecast that my books on sex and family planning would play a small part in altering the sexual behaviour of the British – and even in teaching one or two of them where the clitoris is!

Nor could I have guessed that I would one day be 'prosecuted' by the GMC for writing sex medicine books under my own name and letting my photo appear in women's magazines (heinous crimes in those days); nor indeed could I have forecast that I would fight back, win the case – and eventually be myself elected by the doctors of England to the GMC for fifteen years (an interesting example of poacher turned gamekeeper!).

And as for my recent appearance, in the next column to a topless model, on Page Three of Britain's most disreputable and unreliable newspaper – well, no: I couldn't have foreseen *that* either. . . .

But all of this was a very long way in the future. Right now, on the day I qualified, what I had to do was concentrate on the rat race for houseman's posts at the hospital – posts in which (as newly-qualified doctors) we would be working 130 hours a week in return for a pay packet of eight pounds. The prospect didn't worry me on the day I qualified, because I was feeling extremely cheerful!

I suppose that for a brief moment on that 1960s afternoon, I was tempted into thinking that I'd at last *finished* my long medical training. But, in my heart, I believe I knew that the training had only just begun. . . .

Well, I may be able to tell you what happened to me next – if there's ever a Volume Two.

But *that*, of course, depends on how many people buy Volume One. Please encourage your friends to purchase this book, won't you, dear reader? Times is very, very hard.